**ITS TIME TO UNLOCK YOUR PURPOSE**
**WE HAVE BEEN WAITING LONG ENOUGH**

# I SEE YOU

## Twenty-One-Day Journey to Help You Unlock Your Purpose!

"TIME IS THE ONLY THING YOU CAN NOT GET BACK"

WRITTEN BY Danyelle Dickson
INSPIRE BY YOU.......MY READER

"PEOPLE EVEN MORE THAN THINGS, HAVE TO BE RESTORED, RENEWED, REVIVED, RECLAIMED AND REDEEMED. NEVER THROW OUT ANYONE"
AUDREY HEPBURN

Balboa Press books may be ordered through booksellers or by contacting:

Balboa Press
A Division of Hay House
1663 Liberty Drive
Bloomington, IN 47403
www.balboapress.com
1 (877) 407-4847



Print information available on the last page.

ISBN: 978-1-5043-4228-5 (sc)
ISBN: 978-1-5043-4229-2 (e)

Library of Congress Control Number: 2015916425

Balboa Press rev. date: 11/4/2015

(Don't forget to write down the above statement about you!)

# FOREWORD

**To the men and women who are reading this book:**

**I SEE YOU!**

**If you are feeling lost, isolated, alone, or even empty right now, know that it's only a feeling and your current feelings don't have to be a reality that is rooted in your purpose.**

**I SEE YOU!**

**I want you to recognize that you have been blessed just for being able to hold and read this book no matter how you are feeling right now.**

**I SEE YOU!**

**GOD has truly given you another opportunity to get it right just by gifting you with another day.**

**I SEE YOU!**

**I want you to know....Your greatest gift is another day, and hopefully by the end of this book you will realize that statement and live everyday like it's your last.**

**I SEE YOU!**

I pray this book compels you or better yet inspires you to know: it's not where you've been, or even what you're feeling right now, but it's where you are going.

I SEE YOU!

Today you must uncover and have an unwavering faith that where you are today is exactly where you need to be.

I SEE YOU!

Where you are in life right now is only a small part (but a much needed part) of your journey to completing your purpose.

I SEE YOU!

You may be completely overwhelmed right now.

News flash! YOU AND ONLY YOU are responsible for the status of your life.

But it's not over because YOU AND ONLY YOU can change your life at any time.

EVEN NOW..... TODAY

I SEE YOU!

To change your life WON'T be easy but very necessary.......

You wasted enough time RIGHT?

I AM PERFECTLY AND WONDERFULLY MADE AND POWERFUL BEYOND MEASURE!

(Don't forget to write down the above statement about you!)

**I SEE YOU....**

**I see you for who you really are: perfectly and wonderfully made......here (still living) to accomplish your purpose and to share your purpose with the world.**

**I SEE YOU....**

**Today and every day you have left is the very opportunity you needed to take back your life that you so freely gave up and accomplish your purpose finally.**

**Keep reading.....**

**I pray you will understand all of the *statements made above* by the end of this book.**

**But know:**

**I SEE YOU!**

I AM PERFECTLY AND WONDERFULLY MADE AND POWERFUL BEYOND MEASURE!

---

(Don't forget to write down the above statement about you!)

**"LIVE AS IF YOU WERE TO DIE TOMORROW. LEARN AS IF YOU WERE TO LIVE FOREVER"**

**MAHATMA GANDHI**

______________________________________________

(Don't forget to write down the above statement about you!)

**Contents:**

This book is not a traditional book so there is NO TABLE OF CONTENTS…..NO DEDICATION…..NO PREFACE….REALLY THERE IS NO ORDER…..SO PAY ATTENTION

I wanted you to read my book with an expectation instead of knowing what is coming next while reading.

Just know that the paragraphs of this book were put together by GOD (before I was ever born).

I believed since my gift did not come from me…… but was granted to me…… or better yet gifted to me,

I had to go against the norm and decide to follow my birth-given instructions instead of traditional modern day book requirements.

A little story before the story,

It was suggested to me by multiple friends to change some sentences, grammar and the overall order of the paragraphs in my book before it was published.

One of my friend's works as a professional editor all of them agreed and said…..

You (my reader) would get lost reading my book and recommended for me to get my book professionally edited before my book was released.

(Don't forget to write down the above statement about you!)

They all claimed........ You (my reader) would have a better understanding while reading and my book would have a better flow. My response to their request (to change the order), get the book professionally edited, was........**NO**

Their suggestions quite possibly could be correct.....

Since there are thousands of successful books out there that have proven......it'is necessary to have a proper flow, proper editing, and proper story order, but my answer was still............. **NO.**

This book at times may be hard for you (my reader) to follow...... partly because I wrote this book in two weeks and the words poured out of me like water in no particular order.....

But if I'm really being honest from the start.........Proper English, punctuation, grammar, or story order were **never** really important to me.

I felt my message (my story) to you....... was way more important...... than the order of my stories.

**It's my first book......give me a break.**

So if are an English Teacher get ready.

I really never liked making sure all my sentences contain a noun and a complete thought when I was in school.

I really never cared if I used the proper grammar or the proper sentence tense when I submitted English papers.

______________________________________________

(Don't forget to write down the above statement about you!)

I really really never cared about the order of my stories. I guess I was always rebellious.

While you are reading my book know..........If a lesson was given to me first when I was writing then it was going to come first in my book. **Point blank period**

Don't get me wrong.......I feel all their suggestions are very very important in the school and in Corporate America but not important to my personal purpose being fulfilled by writing **my book** finally.

I threw caution to the wind and stayed true to myself and my writing style.

**Whenever you make a decision to accomplish anything especially out of the norm you will be criticized.**

What they didn't know is their suggestions about my English and my grammar skills were the sole reasons....... I did not sit down and write my book before now.

**Never stop something before it starts** because people see your vision (your purpose) should be carried out in a different manner then you do.

Be willing to be criticized...... I was.............. and still am......

I am the sole editor of this book....So bring it

I thank them all for their suggestions .......and reminded them....... it's not the first time a book was professionally edited and still had a mistake or two.

So I'll give you a hint...

Don't be shock when you are **reading about one thing and I throw in another thought, paragraph, side note, or even a quote**, and go right back to the idea or thought first conveyed.

Please don't be shock if you notice...... I repeat things as you are reading this book.

**Repeating things throughout this book is my attempt to speak to your subconscious mind**.

To me...... if you notice anything repeated they simply were worth repeating.

Pay special attention to the numbered statements, lessons, quotes, or words in **Italics** that will appear throughout the book......

**They are important**..... I promise you.

Some paragraphs at first glance **may not** relate to the section you are reading at the time...... but when you go backwards and read them again.......they will make sense..... **At least I hope!**

This book was designed for you to get what you need when you need it.

I AM PERFECTLY AND WONDERFULLY MADE AND POWERFUL BEYOND MEASURE!

---

(Don't forget to write down the above statement about you!)

**My message to you was way more important to me** than an order of paragraphs or proper sentence structure.

I hope you got your first lesson…..because I got mine…..…..**staying true to myself** was the start of many lessons I learned the moment… ….I decided to write this book to you.

I had to remember and stand on the fact that me being an author had never entered into to my mind until I was 10 years old………and for the record the person that told me I was going to write……. was not the publisher of this book…….my friends……..or the professional editor.

I was told about my writing assignment by GOD ……. so if they(my friends and the professional editor) were not there when he told me…… why should I allow them to alter his plan………..**that was free but equally important.**

STOP……………for a moment!

I want you to STOP reading right now………and start thinking

What person talked you out of completing your purpose before you started working on it?

I want to ask you some questions……Really think about your answers

1. First…Who was there…. when that vision (your purpose) was given to you?

(Don't forget to write down the above statement about you!)

2. Second.........Who were the people who talked you out of working on your purpose before now?
3. Third..........Who were the people telling you....your vision (your purpose) would not work?,.......
4. Fourth.........Who were the people who delayed your vision (your purpose) from coming to pass?

I bet my last dollar.....the people I just reminded you of...telling you that your purpose...... your dream....... your idea.........would not work......**were not** even there when your vision was given to you.

Therefore I'm shouting to you.....right now......... in my loudest voice....

THEIR OPINION REALLY **DOESN'T** MATTER.

**KEEP** DOING YOU...... AND FOR SOME OF YOU READING THIS BOOK.....

**START** DOING YOU.......PLEASE!

**CAN I SHARE MY OPINION WITH YOU?**

1. I believe that we were **all** born with a birth-given purpose inside of us at our conception.
2. I believe when we were born........the blueprint codes to complete that purpose were placed inside of our hearts (not our minds).
3. I believe our blueprint completion codes were fresh and unaltered at birth.

(Don't forget to write down the above statement about you!)

4. I believe **our blueprint codes were written out in words that only we could decipher throughout of lives.**
5. I believe our blueprint codes can only be unlocked by the carrier of the code (you) no matter how long it takes.

**Imagine with me.........**

Imagine......the day you were born...... your very own purpose completion codes were already placed inside of you......

1. The code to unlock every dream you will ever have
2. The code to unlock every idea you will ever have
3. The code to unlock every new business you will ever start
4. The code to unlock every purpose you will ever receive or complete in your entire life.......were already placed in your heart (not your mind).

If you believe me...... and you already had your purpose completion codes inside of you....... then you may be asking.........Danyelle what happened?

Here's what happen ....... You started to **believe** and **accept a very false** image of who you really are.

At birth you knew.....without a shadow of doubt...... you were perfectly and wonderfully made...... nothing was missing and nothing was lacking.

At birth...... you knew the power of your sound........ You would cry....... when you needed to be held, changed, or just when you wanted some attention.

I AM PERFECTLY AND WONDERFULLY MADE AND POWERFUL BEYOND MEASURE!

____________________________________________________________

(Don't forget to write down the above statement about you!)

Think back to all the power you had as a baby....

Who taught you how to cry......to get what you wanted?
No one did........ You just knew and exercised your power freely.

Babies are smaller than anyone in the house but can bring tears to a grown man's face.........., cause a mother to stand still over a crib for hours......just to hear her baby breathing.....

The entire house changes when a baby is born......., even a dog or cat...... take notice of a new baby, and instantly act different...... when a baby is around.

<u>**WOW the power of a baby.......THE POWER OF YOU**</u>

Have you ever before now.....just stopped and recognized what power you had as a baby or even as a toddler?

Some of you are much much older and you still have your parents wrapped around your little finger.

Some of you today......are still using your power........... But...... some of you....<u>**unfortunately are not**</u>.

That same power you had <u>**then**</u>.... Is the very same power you have <u>**now**</u>......

Let's be clear......I'm not saying cry for want you want .....But what I am saying is....... to take the <u>**action necessary**</u> to receive what you want.

I AM PERFECTLY AND WONDERFULLY MADE AND POWERFUL BEYOND MEASURE!

(Don't forget to write down the above statement about you!)

**My Beliefs.....Think about this......**

I feel when we are little children it's the purest time to record and proclaim our purpose in life.

Think about the magic that happens when a child is allowed to speak freely and explore their inner feelings as they grow up.....

Think about the 7 year old that is asked....."**What do you want to be when you grow up?"**

That 7 year old child instantly would boldly state their purpose..... PRESIDENT, ASTRONAUT, MOVIE STAR, ACTOR, FIREMAN, POLICE OFFICER, SINGER, WHATEVER COMES TO THEIR MIND....

That 7 year old will speak their purpose into existence to whomever WITHOUT FEAR or knowhow.

This process (saying what you want to be without fear) is really special to me.....

I asked my 5 year grandson Trayvonn "**what do you want to be when you grow up**"

He instantly said "I want to be NBA Basketball player like Labron James and buy you a house Na Na ..."Wow...he was 5.

They **don't know how** or even what it takes to accomplish their purpose........but they already know........what they think they want to be and are not scared to say it.

I AM PERFECTLY AND WONDERFULLY MADE AND POWERFUL BEYOND MEASURE!

---

(Don't forget to write down the above statement about you!)

It's that boldness feeling (to say what you want to be no matter what) that's the feeling I'm talking about.

It's that same boldness feeling......I want you to remember you already have inside of you, unlock and reclaim before you finish reading my book.

Remember......you are the only one that has the completion codes to unlock your purpose.... **ONLY YOU**

So you may be thinking.......

Danyelle.......How do I unlock my completion codes? Thanks for asking

1. First......You have to be able to look in the mirror and love the person you see starring back..... No matter what you have gone through in life.
2. Second.....You have to state out of your mouth... "I'm ready to unlock my personal codes.....so I can release my purpose to the world.
3. Third.......You have to know your purpose is needed in this world
4. Fourth.....You have to give so that your purpose can come to pass
5. Fifth.........You have to show others love

**Back to my point (no clear order)......I warned you**

**So what happened to you?**

I AM PERFECTLY AND WONDERFULLY MADE AND POWERFUL BEYOND MEASURE!

---

(Don't forget to write down the above statement about you!)

What happen to you?...... is generally what ends up happening to most children...... who are not allowed to boldly proclaim their purpose and follow their inner power from the start or their lives.

You as a child were taught, programmed, at an early age to go with the flow and right then your original purpose codes were altered.

When you go with the flow instead of what's in your heart...... your purpose blue print codes have been faded a little as you keep living...... and for some of you.......your blueprint codes were folded up completely and put up for years.

**STAY WITH ME HERE.....**

Because your purpose blueprint codes were altered by society...... you will need to take baby steps to regain your power you abandoned the moment you let your mind lead you instead of your heart.

Your altered blueprint codes may be **the sole reason** why your purpose has not been presented to the world yet.

You like so many others have been....... looking and listening to the wrong people.

**Today....... marks the day you stop.**

Once your purpose completion blueprint codes were altered as a child or even as an adult.... a chain reaction called life hits......, other people expectations are programmed into your mind .......and BAM......

Your purpose gets pushed **deeper and deeper** down into your subconscious mind.

Until one day……

1. You start to remember…… what you wanted to do in life…..
2. You start to remember…… what you wanted to be in life…….
3. You start to remember……what dream you had the night before…….,
4. You start to hopefully……. stay fixated on a positive thought….. Instead of your negative memories of your past…….,
5. You start to recognize……your uneasy feeling that you should be doing something else with your life.

I hope and pray this book helps……. you unlock every lock door, and leads you to acknowledging your very own personal blueprint codes……you have been ignoring for so long.

This book was designed to propel you to get off your butt and do what you were born to do.

I don't want you to think about **<u>the how</u>** right now……. But just know

1. You have everything you need……. already inside of you
2. You and only you have the codes….. required to unlock your purpose
3. You are still living…….. so you still have time

(Don't forget to write down the above statement about you!)

4. You have to believe .......it's time for your purpose.....to come to pass.

But you like so many others have been thinking yourself **right out** of the vision or idea that was given to you so long ago.

**IT'S TIME TO STOP!**

Let's talk about me....... because writing this book to you..... unlocked some memories that were suppressed deep down inside of me.

Can you imagine being told that you were going to be a Bestselling Author.....at the age of 10.......but do absolutely nothing about it....... for over 30 years?

**This is my story.........**

I went to a standard school that focused on programing children to be workers like every school in America.

Don't get discouraged....just my belief......There is **no class** taught in school on how to be an Owner of a business or how to present and market your invention.....I'm just saying....

My teacher every once in a while would do this exercise and have all the children stand up and announce to the class what they wanted to be when they grew up.

Every one of my classmates wanted to be the President, a Doctor, an Astronaut, Nurse, Etc.... when it was my turn...their answers

(Don't forget to write down the above statement about you!)

sounded so good and important to me……that I sure **didn't** say……..
**I want to be a Bestselling Author.**

I have to be honest…..I couldn't even write well back then……. and I had already been pegged the student……… who **was not** good in English.

You see back then…… the teacher would tell the whole class what grade you got on a test. There was no privacy in my class what so ever.

She would walk down the aisle and you could hear the grades in the background like someone was on a bull horn.

Jessica A, Mark A, Chris B, Michelle C……. as she got closer to me……I prayed…….let her suddenly lose her voice or let the bell ring……please just place my paper face down and keep on walking…… but you know she didn't.

Danyelle you got a D again, it seem like her voice was louder than before or maybe the classroom got quieter.

I'm not sure…..but I heard the chuckles from all the other students so I would not say a word; I just took my paper and hung my head a low as it would go.

So needless to say…….when my teacher asked me…..What I wanted to be when I grew up…..I sure didn't tell the truth.

**I WANT TO BE A BESTSELLING AUTHOR**,………..I should have screamed just as loud as she announced my D………**but I didn't**

(Don't forget to write down the above statement about you!)

The Truth is.........**I went with the norm** and said a Nurse. Hat's off to nurses, but I couldn't even stand the sight of blood...... not even at 10.

I was standing there....... telling **a bold face lie** to myself, the teacher, and my peers.

**Side Note:** When you lie about who you really are to other people...... you are especially lying to yourself first.........from that point on...... because of your lies......you are delaying your purpose from becoming a reality.

**Back to me for a moment........**

What I'm trying to say is.....I lied to fit in with my class.

I didn't want be laughed at, and I surly didn't want to draw attention to myself.......... after I just got a D on my English paper......... **Non-the-less it was still a lie.**

If you are doing the same thing today (lying) for whatever reason...... by the end of my book I pray you stop......lying finally.

Is this section....... where you are in your life right now?

1. Are you not doing your purpose because you don't want to go against the norm?
2. Are you not doing your purpose because you were told what to do by your parents, or maybe you are doing what you said out of your mouth instead of what was in your heart?

(Don't forget to write down the above statement about you!)

3. Are you not doing your purpose because you just lying to fit in?
4. Are you not doing your purpose because you are lying to yourself?
5. **You only have one life, not two, and it's time to do what you were born to do.**

I wanted to be a Bestselling Author, when I was shown the vision by GOD, it felt right to me.

I was already keeping a diary and I was already writing every day.

So what I wasn't good in English.....**Did it really matter?**

How many people are successful in a field that they **were not** initially good at?

The vision was given to me before I was **ever** in English class....

My vision **never** changed even after...... I received bad grades in English.

I still knew deep deep down inside of me......I wanted to be a Bestselling Author more then I wanted to be anything else in life.

So.......if writing felt right to me.......and I was already was keeping a diary.........,
I wrote my first play at 9........ You tell me why when I was given the opportunity to speak me being a Bestselling Author into existence in front of my English class....... I didn't.

(Don't forget to write down the above statement about you!)

Me not telling my teacher and my classmates who I really was on that day cost me sooooo much.......

Me lying on that day......suppressed my bestselling author feelings.........delayed this book........and delayed my birth given purpose.

Don't make the same mistake I did........... It cost me 30 years.

The reality is......... we all have to pay some price for the decisions we make.

Not being true to yourself.......will always cost you something.

1. For some people....... lies cost them sleepless nights,
2. For some people....... lies cost them health,
3. For some people....... lies cost them happiness
4. For some people....... lies even cost them death.

**YOU HAVE LIFE**.....So...... if you are reading this book.

You need to **finally** realize that your cost has already been **PAID IN FULL.....**

If your purpose hasn't come to pass yet, the time you have wasted is your cost.

Not living life for you is **all**.......you will ever have to pay.

You have already **PAID THE PRICE IN FULL.....**

I AM PERFECTLY AND WONDERFULLY MADE AND POWERFUL BEYOND MEASURE!

---

(Don't forget to write down the above statement about you!)

Your un-filled purpose or dream will not cost you anything else...... because today is a new day and another opportunity for you to get it right.

Every day now.......... is your opportunity to do what you were born to do.

**Now keep reading.... I'm just getting started.**

**Wow!**

While writing this section that memory came up (that was a 30 year old memory).

That memory made me realize how much time I personally wasted...... living from the point of my mind instead of living from the point of my heart.

That memory made me realize.........how thankful I am to still be living and able to write this book to you.

**So again..... Does sentence structure or order really matter?**

If you really want to unlock your purpose then know......

**There is power in speaking your purpose into existence no matter what age you are**.

Even though I did not speak my writing purpose into existence back then......I have always been provided a platform to speak and help others.............. which has always been a personal goal of mine.

(Don't forget to write down the above statement about you!)

For some reason.......I have always been placed in the front of the room speaking and encouraging people to do their very best.....I can honestly say......... I have always had a platform to be heard.

I told people that same English teacher story....but back then I simply focused on the fact that....... I was not being truthful to myself.......and me not being able to speak life into my very own purpose cost me so much.

When I shared that story publicly...... I never before now..... Realized the fact that I was already programmed (not to speak the truth) by the age of 10.

WOW. Looking back, I never focused on the **real truth** that experience taught me before writing this section to you.

That day was an important moment in my life......it was **that day... ....**I decided and accepted my normal person program stamp.

It was **that day** ......I went the norm instead of what was in my heart.

It was **that day** my author blueprint code was folded up and put away for over 30 years;

It was **that day** that I did not have the boldness to say what was in my heart.

It was **that day**........life began to hit me like a ton of bricks.

**When was your day?**

I AM PERFECTLY AND WONDERFULLY MADE AND POWERFUL BEYOND MEASURE!

___

(Don't forget to write down the above statement about you!)

Do you have a memory of **the day** when........ You didn't say what was in your heart?

Do you have a memory of **the day** when you shared your purpose or idea and it was not received well...... so you thought your purpose was not meant to be?

That's **the day** in my opinion when you became **NORMAL** and learned to go with the flow.

I think it takes an **un-normal person** in this world...... to make a difference.

I believe that there are millions or people walking around with a NORMAL stamp on their forehead.

Millions of people are walking around scared to follow their heart instead of their minds.

There is a real difference in people who let their **heart lead** them and people who let their **mind lead** them.

Then there is....... you.......

TODAY .....You ARE pulling that NORMAL stamp right off YOUR FOREHEAD and deciding to recognize the mistakes **I made in my life**....... and **finally do what you were born to do.**

**Let's be clear.... I want you to get this... Back to me for a moment**

(Don't forget to write down the above statement about you!)

I would tell everybody who would listen….."**Time is the only thing you cannot get back**" but I **wasn't** living what I was teaching.

I was teaching people about time management skills….pushing people to their destiny……stressing the importance of following their hearts…….and the reality was this book….my book……wasn't even written yet.

If you are not careful the same thing will happen to you.

You will start to simply exist…….. instead of living your life to the fullest. There is a HUGE difference.

It took years to re-program myself (don't get paranoid on me) all I mean is….it years for me to finally speak and do what I was born to do…… instead of what my mouth and mind wanted me to do.

Needless to say…….speaking what people wanted to hear about me instead of…. who I really was……. lead me down a path of feeling unfulfilled for over 30 years.

No matter how much success or praise I got in life. The praise never really filled the void I felt on a daily.

I wasn't doing what GOD showed me I was born to do (writing)…… so my nights were very long and restless.

I'm no doctor but I feel we all have triggers, well I call them triggers…… what I mean is…… all of us from time to time…..will feel or exhibit symptoms…..when we are not doing what we were born to do.

I AM PERFECTLY AND WONDERFULLY MADE AND POWERFUL BEYOND MEASURE!

---

(Don't forget to write down the above statement about you!)

My first trigger #1 identified **Sleepless Nights**

I could never sleep through the entire night. I would wake up every night between 2:00-3:00am without an alarm….. I would just wake up.

I accepted my trigger which was my biggest mistake. Instead of dealing with the root problem……I again went with the flow.

**Accepting instead of dealing with**…..Here is an example of my mistake

Since I knew I was going to wake up anyway……and I was tired of hitting my baby toe on the bed trying to walk around in the dark….. I would fall asleep every night with a book in my lap.

So when I woke up…… I would just start right back reading again… ..I did not have to get out of bed or wake up my husband.

Whenever you are not really dealing with a symptom (trigger) you always search for someone who has the same problem as you.

One of the books I read every night was the Bible.

I found comfort in one story, the story of Samuel.

The story showed me…… that if I was waking up at night…… maybe GOD wanted to speak to me……just like he spoke to Samuel.

Just in case you don't know this story…….

Samuel was sleeping one night in one room…Eli was sleeping in another room… and they were the only ones in this house.

(Don't forget to write down the above statement about you!)

In the middle of the night Samuel heard someone call his name so naturally he went to Eli and said yes you called me........but Eli replied.... I did not call you.

Eli told Samuel to go back to bed..... Samuel at this point did not know GOD...... so nothing in his mind would have thought......... GOD was trying to speak to him.

Samuel went to go back to bed and again he heard GOD call his name.....and again Samuel went to Eli and said yes........ you called me .......

But this time Eli realized GOD was trying to speak to Samuel and told him to go back....., lie down......but when you hear the voice of GOD again reply....... speak Lord your servant is listening.

Then GOD spoke to Samuel and revealed some secret things that were going to happen to Eli and his two sons. The moment I read this story I taught maybe GOD is trying to speak to me.

I told you...... I was accepting my trigger..... not dealing with the root cause of why I could not sleep through the night.

If you are having the same problem of not sleeping through the night.... have you ever considered;

1. When you can't sleep..... maybe.....GOD is trying to speak to you
2. When you can't sleep......maybe...... GOD is trying to get your attention because when you are awake you will not listen.

I AM PERFECTLY AND WONDERFULLY MADE AND POWERFUL BEYOND MEASURE!

---

(Don't forget to write down the above statement about you!)

3. When you can't sleep...... maybe.......GOD is trying to give you instructions

There are a lot more reasons possibly why you can't sleep through the night but we are talking about me........................so I want you to **stay focused** right here.

I instantly thought GOD wanted to speak to me.....So every night instead of reading again when I woke up........ I would just lie quiet and say speak GOD.

I would listen quietly sometimes for hours......... GOD did speak to me some nights...... but the talk was more about what I was going through at the time.

The conversation about me being an author was last on GOD's list.......

GOD thankfully would speak to me...... about my current life problems at the time.

My life had become too crazy for him to remind me of writing.

I needed direction that only GOD could give to me.

I told you...... life had hit me like a ton of bricks.

I wasn't lying there were days....man........all I can say is ......there were days

(Don't forget to write down the above statement about you!)

I'm so thankful GOD came to the circumstance a hand instead of reminding me of being an Author. I was not ready yet

1. I needed to forgive
2. I needed to love
3. I needed to have compassion
4. I needed to have self-control
5. I needed GOD

I needed all those things.....before I could ever write this book to you.

My spirit was thankfully was being filled.....however my mind was still racing.

To tell you the truth.......... I still was not sleeping through the night.

Some of you reading this book right now......are experiencing the same problem.......you are not sleeping through the night.

I'm no doctor........but I told you........ I think sleepless nights are a trigger that you **may not** be doing what you were born to do.....or maybe you **are not** walking in your truth.

Answer these questions for me.

1. Are you personally denying a truth about your current situation
2. Are you denying yourself in any way?
3. Are you needing to forgive

(Don't forget to write down the above statement about you!)

4. Are you needing to show love
5. Are you needing to have self- control

In order to be gifted the opportunity to finally fulfill your purpose in life you must first ask yourself the above questions

**Keep reading......my mind was still racing and I still could not sleep**

If I told my doctor about me not being able to sleep........

He would say "I was under stress or maybe I was suffering from Insomnia" and try to prescribe me some medication.

No matter who I turned to....... they all had an answer to ........why I was not sleeping.

I'm proud of myself ......because I didn't start taking any medication and I didn't listen to everybody who had an opinion about my sleeping problem.

**Side note; don't listen to everybody opinions about your situation or problem......... learn to listen to you.**

I want you to know....... the day I started writing this book to you was the first day..... I slept through the entre night.

Sleeping through the night....WOW........some people take for granted....... WELL.....I don't.

(Don't forget to write down the above statement about you!)

I attribute me being gifted rest and sleeping peacefully through the entire night..... To me fulfilling my purpose........of writing this book to you.

I believe if you are having problems sleeping...... you may **not** be accepting a truth about yourself. Learn how to listen to you and walk into the truth...don't run from it.

Through the years I had to learn to appreciate all my triggers and I'm telling you to do the same thing if you want to complete your purpose.

The moment I wasn't doing or saying what GOD called me to be doing or saying...... once again my sleepless nights would return.

**A sleepless night was a great trigger for me.**

Imagine....... every time you did anything that was not pleasing or every time you got off path in any way........you could not sleep through the night.

I was so thankful I recognized my trigger and knew I was off my purpose completing path.

I would do whatever I had to do...... to get back to sleeping peacefully through the night. (This usually meant apologizing for my behavior to someone)

Another great trigger for me was headaches.

---

(Don't forget to write down the above statement about you!)

Every time I did anything that I was not called to do ...**BAM!** I instantly got a headache

I don't know if you are experiencing some of the same things (sleepless nights or headaches) however when you are not doing what you were born to do...... your body will tell you........in some form or fashion. **(Again my opinion)**

Some of you reading this book right now.......are experiencing headaches, sleepless nights, pains, dreams, visions, and you are running around.....like a chicken with its head cut off......telling doctors, teachers, family members, and who ever else will listen about the symptoms you are experiencing.

**STOP IT.**

The people you are telling about your symptoms are at a disservice.......because they have no idea what you are really thinking.........or aspiring to be deep down inside.

They are naturally speaking to or treating the symptom....... instead of your **root cause...... Which could be you simply are denying a truth about the real you.**

**What if......What they are telling you is wrong?**

**What if........ All you ever had to do...... was start working on your purpose** and the symptoms would stop?

**I'm not telling you to stop** listening to medical doctors but what I am telling you..... to **start listening to you.**

I AM PERFECTLY AND WONDERFULLY MADE AND POWERFUL BEYOND MEASURE!

---

(Don't forget to write down the above statement about you!)

You have a great power inside of you......to do whatever you want to do.

You also have the power to command sickness and disease to leave your body......

**YOU ARE THAT POWERFUL**

**DISCLAIMER: IM NOT A DOCTOR**

**SO PLEASE DON'T STOP SPEAKING TO DOCTORS.**

**THIS IS JUST MY STORY.**

**DON'T TAKE THIS SECTION AS MEDICAL ADVICE IN ANYWAY**

**THIS IS REALLY........ JUST MY STORY, MY TRUTH.**

By the end of this book......I know you will be working on your purpose daily.... so PLEASE write me or let me know by email at **successwithdanyelle@gmail.com**.......if the moment you started speaking positive, forgiving yourself and started working on your purpose....... if your trigger stopped.......like mine did.

Write me and tell me what changed for you....... when you decided to live your life for the reason you were born........................... instead of living for others.

**That was one of those side thoughts that are out of order.**

I AM PERFECTLY AND WONDERFULLY MADE AND POWERFUL BEYOND MEASURE!

______________________________________________________________

(Don't forget to write down the above statement about you!)

**Back to my lesson,**

I had to stand on the lesson I learned at 10 years old and the real fact that I was tired of having sleepless nights.

**My requirements of you……While reading my book!**

1. Please read this book with an open mind and more importantly and better yet an expectation that you are going to receive everything you need to rocket launch you to completing your purpose finally.
2. Please learn from all of my countless mistakes outline in this book
3. Please learn to accept yourself.
4. Please learn to relate to the analogies placed throughout this book
5. Please learn the value of your time.

This book was designed to propel you to complete your purpose finally or……if nothing less this book will speak positive things into your life about your destiny….

***So does the order of words or paragraphs throughout this book really matter?***

As long as you read with an astounding expectation that you are going to get the steps required to unlock your purpose……..then by the end of this book.

**I promise you will.**

(Don't forget to write down the above statement about you!)

Promise is a strong word ...... Yea......... but**...... I STILL PROMISE**

I'm simply promising that **your positive expectation** overshadows any words contained in my book.

**Your positive expectation** overshadows your current situation and really overshadows your past.

If you truly believe that something contained in this book is the key to unlocking your purpose then **you will receive** the steps. It's that simple

I wrote this book **not to** make any claims.
I wrote this book because my birth-given purpose was to write.
I wrote this book to convey to you in writing...... that you **still have time.**
I wrote this book to leave **a legacy of love**
I wrote this book to say the following:

To: YOU (MY READER)

To: MY CHILDREN

To: MY CHILDREN'S CHILDREN

To: THE WORLD AS A WHOLE

*I SEE YOU.....*

*I LOVE YOU.....*

I AM PERFECTLY AND WONDERFULLY MADE AND POWERFUL BEYOND MEASURE!

________________________________________

(Don't forget to write down the above statement about you!)

*I BELIEVE IN YOU.....*

*I SEE YOU AS MY FAMILY MEMBER......*

*I SEE WHAT YOU WENT THROUGH....AND IT DID NOT BREAK YOU.*

*I SEE YOU STILL HAVE TIME LEFT AND CAN ACCOMPLISH THAT WHICH YOU WERE BORN TO ACCOMPLISH......*

*I SEE THE REAL YOU AND KNOW YOU DO HAVE A PURPOSE....*

*I SEE A PURPOSE THAT NO ONE CAN GIVE TO YOU.....AND NO ONE CAN TAKE AWAY......*

*I SEE THE REAL YOU....AND YOU ALONE....*

*PLEASE READ THIS BOOK WITH AN EXPECTATION OF RECEIVING STEPS TO UNLOCKING YOUR PURPOSE....*

*AND THOSE VERY STEPS WILL BE CONTAINED IN THIS BOOK....*

**"KNOWING IS NOT ENOUGH**
**WE MUST APPLY**
**WILLING IS NOT ENOUGH WE MUST DO"**
**BRUCE LEE**

**REMEMBER** order was not really important to me......here's an example....They thought this should have been the start of my book. **You have to admit what you read so far was good.**

(Don't forget to write down the above statement about you!)

There are so many great books in the world today so I want to thank you first for reading mine. I initially wanted to create a short page book designed especially for you (my reader)..... My family member's world-wide.

The book your about to finish reading was originally short for two reasons.

The first reason....... and I have to be real honest from the start... simply put.....

I kind of get bored when reading long paged books and go figure..... my book ended up being longer than I expected.

Truly, I do believe reading is fundamental; however I have too many friends that started books and never finished them, or like me had a book marks in 5 or 6 different books at the same time.

If......I'm being real honest

**I did not want to be an author who wrote a book that was not read to the end**.

So read my book to the end...... there is a special ending designed just for you.

Don't get me wrong......

Today, I'm proud to say........ I finish all the books I start..... NOW

(Don't forget to write down the above statement about you!)

However reading books to the end was not something I practiced throughout the years. **I told you I get bored fast.**

**I wasn't lying**

Looking back over **all** my reading experiences.......after I made a vow to myself to appreciate everything that came across my path in my life, reading a book to the end, has become one of my personal goals.

The second reason my book was going to be short was for two more reasons,

Number one of the second reason is that........

**I simply wanted you to finish my book**. Smile please.....

Number two of my second reason.... is because experts say.....if you do anything consistently every day for 21 days then it becomes a habit.

So in my mind......I imagined you living the 21 sayings outlined at the end of this book.... I was compelled to write about you and one day you would email me....at **successwithdanyelle@gmail.com.**

I need you to tell me how this book helped you unlocked the required doors in your mind and your purpose was finally completed!

I literally wanted this book to only be 21 pages but they would not publish a book that small. (I tried)

I AM PERFECTLY AND WONDERFULLY MADE AND POWERFUL BEYOND MEASURE!

---

(Don't forget to write down the above statement about you!)

So since my book had to be longer than I expected……God showed me visions through my stories and analogies placed in my book……. that I had to include to get you ready to receive the 21 sayings located at the end of this book…..**I love it when a plan comes together.**

When you get to that 21 day section located at the end my book… ….I pray the steps outlined (connected with your belief) finally unleashes your purpose to the world.

**The steps are towards the back of this book……. so keep reading.**

When you get to those 21 day steps……

1. Promise me…… that you will try to believe the words you read every day.
2. Promise me that you will remember the stories and analogies you read before you got to that section
3. Promise me that you will do the work required to change your life.

If you read the sayings, write the sayings, and do action towards your purpose daily….MAN…….. **NO ONE WILL BE ABLE TO STOP YOU. Not even you!**

I'll let you in on a little secret…… while you are reading, writing and speaking the positive words about yourself every day for 21 days……. you will be working and accomplishing your purpose by default.

**I told you no clear order but I warned you…… so keep reading**

(Don't forget to write down the above statement about you!)

**Where was I? OH reading books to the end!**

It took me a while to read a book to the end......but I still strongly encourage you to always finish the books you start.

So defiantly finish mine first.....

Then go back to the books you have lying all around the house........ and make it a point to finish what you started.

Why? Because out of all the books in the world...... you bought that book.......and there is something in that very book for you.

I don't know what it is.......but I know..... It's in there.

You see.......there is a powerful connection between you and all the things that come into your life...... even books.

However you obtained that book whether you purchase the book or received as a gift..... I believe there is something in that very book for you.

Think back for a moment......to when you first got the books you currently have.

Were you are feeling like something in your **life was missing**?

You had to be **searching** for something when that book came to you right?

(Don't forget to write down the above statement about you!)

The key or answer to your questions does not always appear in books because sad to say not every one reads books.

The key or answer to **your questions** may come in a song, a TV show, or even a radio show....... but one thing is for sure...... if you ask a question.......... **the answer will always be revealed to you in some way**

For this section......I only want you to consider all the books in your presence right now......including mine.

Think back to all the books you have lying around your house or office.

**WHY DID YOU BUY THE BOOK?**

Was it something that caught your eye on the book cover?
Was it the title?
Was it something that you read in the book?
Was it the back cover picture?
Was the book recommended?
What caught your eye about that book?

If you bought the book then something in you.....immediately thought the book contained the **very answer**......you **were looking** for......

I have to get deep right here.

It does not matter the reason you consciously or sub-consciously bought the book.

(Don't forget to write down the above statement about you!)

I'm saying without a shadow of a doubt ......if you bought the book.....I automatically believe there was something in that very book for you.

You may be thinking.......Danyelle I have read some books and I didn't get anything out of.

Well..... I'm telling you...... **the answer was in there**.......... but..... maybe you missed it.

I believe all our answers.....we will ever need or ask....... will always be given to us........in some form.

**(Repeat yes) it's important.**

For now...... I'm just talking about all your books...... even mine

Let's just say for the record you **didn't** get anything out of the book you bought or read.........Consider this.

Could it be maybe...... you didn't read the book with an expectation to receive what you needed

Could it be....... maybe you didn't want to read through the little things you felt you didn't need....... to get to the things in the book......that you did need.

Sometimes in a 1000 page book...... there could only be **one line** that unlocks the door to your purpose or provide the very answer to your question.

---

(Don't forget to write down the above statement about you!)

You are LOVED sooooooo much .......that you will always receive your answers....... to every question you will ever ask.............. ALWAYS

Take on my belief system for a moment

I believe............ there is a powerful connection........between you the reader...... and the writer of a book.

I feel this way about every book that was ever written.

I believe that an Author had a specific reader in mind before he or she ever sat down and wrote their book.

I feel the very same way about my book.......

You see....... I wrote this book....... but...... I attached my personal positive power to my writing.......

I willed that every hurt person or better yet....... every person who had not accomplished their purpose yet ......would pick up my book someday and finally complete and release their purpose to the world

And guess what........ **YOU DID.**

Please don't let anything deter you from reading to this book to the end.

If you cannot finish my book....... promise me then......that you will read my book until you find your one line, your section, or even the answer to what you thought you needed before this book ever crossed your path.

I hope this book will somehow point out the importance of you listening to you……

**YOU ARE GREAT AND WORTH LISTENING TO……….**

Not only do I want you…….to start listening to you…… but I need you to start analyzing everything that has ever crossed your path in the past…….and especially from this day forward analyze everything that will ever cross your path in the future.

Nothing shows up in your life (either positive or negative) unless you willed it into existence.

**YOU ARE THAT POWERFUL**

I need you to start recognizing and following your own inner voice.

Listening to your inner voice……..is a vital key to unlocking your purpose

Let me finish my story……

After I obtain the courage to write this book my attention quickly went to back to all the books and pages I read in my lifetime.

Sometimes as many as 3000 pages…..not to mention I read the Bible from cover to cover twice.

I AM PERFECTLY AND WONDERFULLY MADE AND POWERFUL BEYOND MEASURE!

(Don't forget to write down the above statement about you!)

At first glance...... I wasn't sure why....... I went back to my personal reading experiences........so I did what my inner self lead me to do.

I took out all the books, every book that was on my book shelf, and every book that was just lying around my house.

I noticed the moment I saw a book cover ......all I could ever remember about the book was a very small portion.

Don't ask me what the whole book was about because I would not be able to tell you.

One thing remained true with every book I ever read in my life.

I would only retain the most important lesson or only remembered the part of the book that related to me the most.

When I first noticed...... I did that with all books.... it was weird. I asked myself all the time.

**Really Danyelle out of all the words in that book you only remember that part**.

At first it bothered me ........It was serious problem for me.....

I thought "**does that make me is selfish or what**"?

Has this ever happened to you?

I cannot be the only one...... in this entire world.....that had these same feelings when reading books.

(Don't forget to write down the above statement about you!)

My problems……..

1. I got bored fast reading long paged books
2. I did not finish all the books I started
3. I could only remember the part of the book that was most important to me

I told you the words of this book poured out of me like water when I started writing in no particular order but as I wrote these words and really thought about my personal reading experiences…..

IT hit me….I got it….I got why…… I would not change my sentence structure, order of paragraphs or get my book professionally edited.

**I GOT IT!**

I asked myself **"what part in my book would be the most important to you (my reader)".** I didn't know what line would be important to you…..

**I love it when GOD's plan is revealed.**

The order of my book didn't matter to me……… but……. the ordered of my book mattered to me completing my purpose……… and following my inner instruction not outer peoples requirements.

You see……I didn't know your reading patterns……… I didn't know if you got bored reading long page books like me, and I really didn't know if you finished all the books that you started.

**SO I JUST HAD TO**……. Give love in the beginning of my book just in case you only got to the first page,

I AM PERFECTLY AND WONDERFULLY MADE AND POWERFUL BEYOND MEASURE!

---

(Don't forget to write down the above statement about you!)

**I WAS REQUIRED TO..**,....Give a story before the story just in case you did to get to the rest of my book.

**I WAS INSTRUCTED TO......**keep this order...... completely out of order.......just for you (MY READER).

I had to include analogies that only you can relate to. (You will get to them shortly)

I had to repeat things....... when I'm stressing an important concept or thought.......You (my reader) will not get lost reading my book because........ I know **you needed me** to stress that specific point.

It goes back to my statement....... if you are holding or reading this book right now then........there **is** something in this book just for you!

**Key: When you are shown visions......don't question them! Just do what it takes to bring the vison to the surface.**

**Don't be afraid to look at yourself when mapping out your purpose.**

**Remember you have everything in you already to accomplish your vision.**

**I have to be honest again ..... You should know by now...... honesty is important to me.**

The moment you are given a vision.......we can't help but to look at ourselves............ however...................please learn from my mistakes.

I AM PERFECTLY AND WONDERFULLY MADE AND POWERFUL BEYOND MEASURE!

---

(Don't forget to write down the above statement about you!)

If you have to glance at a snap-shot of yourself when you are given a vision.......then up-front..........

I want **you** to automatically **exclude your current situation.**

I revealed earlier in my book......that you were born with your purpose.........and have everything you need to accomplish your purpose already inside of you right.

**Does your current situation even matter?**

**NO**

If you haven't fulfilled your purpose yet...... then know...... it doesn't matter what you have gone through....... Or even.......what you are in right now today.

**It's your time......**This is what I teach.

1. I teach never look in the mirror until you can truly see positive things staring back at you.
2. I teach.....You have to learn to see who you really are regardless..... to what you think see physically or emotionally
3. I teach .....You can always make the required changes to unlock what is locked inside of you.
4. I teach.........You **are not** your current situation..........you are **way more** powerful than your current situation.
5. I teach....You are not who your past says you are....You are **way more** powerful than your past.

I AM PERFECTLY AND WONDERFULLY MADE AND POWERFUL BEYOND MEASURE!

______________________________________________

(Don't forget to write down the above statement about you!)

When you read those words **(YOU ARE POWERFUL)** did you believe them?

**ITS TRUE**.......However, I have to be honest what generally ends up happening........ is you stay stuck looking at yourself in the mirror......... and start to believe the false image of who **you think** you are.......solely based on your current situation or even based on your past.

That's a mistake millions of people make.

Holding onto the false image of their current circumstance prevents them from acting on the vision that was given to them at birth.

In this book....... you will be required to finally **stop creating** things....... you **do not** want.

You and you alone....are the **sole reason** for where your life is today

In order to get to your purpose you have to promise me from this day forward.......that you will **never give up** on your vision....... until your purpose comes to pass.

No matter what your personal situation is today! I need you to..... **Think**, **Imagine**, **See** your purpose as already happening, and then just **speak** it into existence.

1. See it
2. Speak it
3. Watch it come to pass

I AM PERFECTLY AND WONDERFULLY MADE AND POWERFUL BEYOND MEASURE!

(Don't forget to write down the above statement about you!)

If there is something that you have been shown (YOUR PURPOSE) then that's what you should spend your time working on……period.

Don't ever question if you are the person that should bring your purpose to pass

**Just do it…….**

The vision was given to you, how to accomplish that vision was also given to you.

Its inside of you…You just have to believe.

***LET'S TALK ABOUT ME………***

For me……… whenever I started to follow GOD's plan for my life and started writing……..it seemed like I was always distracted by my life………. and I never had time to write.

Until one day…… I pushed passed my mess of a life……. that I created……… and I starting writing……….

WOW……

All I can tell you is ……I received an all-consuming good feeling……

**IT WAS ONE THE BEST FEELING OF MY LIFE.**

Writing came easy for me. I wasn't 10 anymore; no one was grading my words.

I AM PERFECTLY AND WONDERFULLY MADE AND POWERFUL BEYOND MEASURE!

(Don't forget to write down the above statement about you!)

I just sat down at a computer and literally wrote this book in about 14 days....I wrote my first book in about 2 days. That book still hasn't been published yet but non- the less I wrote it.

I wasted 33 years of my life staying fixated on my past instead of my promise.

The moment you accept your assignment........and don't question your worth....... that's when everything will start to flow easily.

If it happened for me **it will** happen for you.

Thoughts, ideas, people and money will suddenly be aligned and available to help your purpose come to pass.

Some of you reading this book need to change your focus right now.

You are focused on the wrong things in your life.

**ITS NOT WORKING BOO...TRY SOMETHING NEW FOR ONCE**

Try to focus on...... working on your purpose.......for a period of time.

Follow the steps listed below.......The steps are easier than you think

When you change your focus all types of new things will be revealed to you:

1. Write down what your vision is.....what do you want to accomplish?

---

(Don't forget to write down the above statement about you!)

2. Believe that you are the person that should be doing that vision
3. Take time out of your day.....to sit down, quiet your spirit and listen for instructions.......**this part should be completed every day**
4. Write down what is being downloaded **into you** during those quiet moments
5. Start to research......how do you complete your purpose? (Google is great source) just ask a question and the answer will appear.
6. Do something....work towards completing your purpose every day!

It's really that easy.......how long it takes for people to complete those steps is the hard part.

You see.......Most people will never finish what they start.

**Are you different?**

**YES**

One or all of those steps listed above usually are started..... then life hits....your false self-image of yourself hits......then you go from working towards completing your purpose every day to allowing the negative feelings to overtake you,

When you allow negative feeling **in**........the excitement feelings you had when you first started working on completing your purpose....... are now **out**.

(Don't forget to write down the above statement about you!)

**I need you to be different!**

**Starting today**.....learn how to **appreciate all your feelings** both negative and positive....both good feelings and bad feelings.

I need you to appreciate **all your feelings** in order for this book to work in your life.

**Any feelings** that you receive from this day forward while working on completing your purpose are necessary for you to reach your purpose.

**That's right I said necessary!**

Some of you fail because you constantly question your inner feelings or visions and I'm telling you to.......... **STOP**.

It doesn't matter if your feelings are positive or negative ......

They both will push you to the place of change...... so never question your feelings or your visions....... just because you are feeling a certain way.

**Take a walk with me.......**

Let's just say you are working on completing your purpose...... you are feeling so good about yourself and your new found purpose...... Life is good to you right now

Then one day you get a negative phone call or you run into a person who knows you from your past.

I AM PERFECTLY AND WONDERFULLY MADE AND POWERFUL BEYOND MEASURE!

---

(Don't forget to write down the above statement about you!)

**BAM**........all those old negative feelings came pouring back into you again like a flood.

**What should you do?**

First.....I want you to **thank the person** who called or ran into you and reminded you of all your negative feelings...... because **NOW** you have identified who to **avoid** in the future......... if you are feeling weak.

Second......I want you to **thank yourself** for all those old negative feelings you just thought about.

Third........I want you to **thank yourself** for the person you are today and realize how far you have come.............,

Fourth......I want you to **thank yourself** for life........,

Fifth.........I want you to **move pass** those old feelings and go **right back** to working on completing your purpose.

You must do the above steps every time a negative feeling is brought to you......EVERYTIME.......

**Don't let anyone or any feeling deter you from completing your purpose.**

Back to me for a second.....I told you the words written in this book applied to me first.

**I just thought of something I think will be helpful to you!**

(Don't forget to write down the above statement about you!)

I really did not question the vision (me being author) however I did question myself (MISTAKE #1).

My feelings that I was born to write did not change........ It's hard to explain......

When my old negative feelings came in............I begin to ask GOD questions:

**Why me**?
**Why now**?
**Did I even know how to write**?
**How do I publish a book**?

My greatest question that set me back years....

**Did I even have the ability to write an entire book?**

My writing feelings never left me....but the above questions overshadowed and totally consumed me at times.....

I gave into my feelings (those questions) which delayed me from even sitting down at a computer and writing.

If I would have known the words of both of my books would have poured out of me like water....... all I can say is I would have wrote way more books then the two I wrote so far.

Participating in that negative tug a war.....between my old negative feelings and those questions.....just **wasn't** good for me.

I AM PERFECTLY AND WONDERFULLY MADE AND POWERFUL BEYOND MEASURE!

---

(Don't forget to write down the above statement about you!)

**SO I JUST HAD TO** develop a better plan for you.

Working on completing my purpose daily taught me:

1. To be **thankful** for my past
2. To be **thankful** for my current distractions (kids, work, friends etc.)
3. To be **thankful** for me....even in the mist of the storm,

Just me learning to be thankful for my life and the time I had left..... lead me to practice my writing skills in the midst of the storm.

Writing everyday **has become** a necessary part of my process to survive.

**What process are you doing when something isn't going your way?**

I remember when something wasn't going my way.

I became a master escape artist (never dealing with my root problems) just ran away from my problems all the time.

Every time old negative feelings came up for me.... I sure didn't do the steps outline for you.

**The plan outlined in this book was not written yet.**

My process went like this: (keep in mind my process **didn't** work)

I would go and take a bubble bath, light some candles, play soft music, cry, and have a glass a wine.

Now when I came out of that bathroom..... Sometimes the things were better and sometimes (most of the times) they weren't.

**My process didn't work for years**..........

**SO I JUST HAD TO....**write this book........ for you to have a better process......

You shouldn't have to make the same mistakes I did.

What were the mistakes I made in life for?

I believe all my **dumb mistakes** I made in my life were only to help you.

**WANT A MIND SHIFT CHANGE? Think about this**

1. When you learn from your mistakes...... you **no longer** give power to your mistake
2. When **you don't do** the things you **know don't work**....you return the power **back to you**.
3. When you believe every mistake you **ever made** was done to help someone else.....You stop beating yourself up
4. **You are powerful**....... stop giving your power up for every negative feeling that comes your way......

I wrote this book in 14 days however I was 43 years old when my 14 days started.

This book was published without a doubt with perfect timing........ but I can't help but wonder.....

I AM PERFECTLY AND WONDERFULLY MADE AND POWERFUL BEYOND MEASURE!

---

(Don't forget to write down the above statement about you!)

Where would I be in my life, or better yet who died without ever reading a book design to push them to completing their purpose?

How many people could I have helped if I would have wrote my book when I first got the feeling that I was going to be a bestselling author........over 30 years ago.

Something to think about.........

**Time is the only thing you cannot get back.....SO STOP...... wasting your time.**

**Repeat on purpose.......I need you to get this**

First.....I want you to realize not everything is going to go your way....all the time.......and it's OK.
Second.....I want you to deal with your root problems instead of avoiding the true cause of why you are feeling a certain way.
Third.... I want you to do whatever you have to do .......to make it right and get back to working on completing your purpose
Fourth........I want you to make working on your purpose...... a part of your healing process
Fifth........I want you to go right back to working on completing your purpose

You must do those steps every time a negative feeling is brought to you......EVERYTIME.......

1. Remember to use this exercise every time something doesn't go your way.......

I AM PERFECTLY AND WONDERFULLY MADE AND POWERFUL BEYOND MEASURE!

---

(Don't forget to write down the above statement about you!)

2. Learn how to make working on your purpose a part of that process that gets you through those bad thoughts and feelings.

**MY LESSON.......**

When GOD gave me the vision.......my attention was quickly drawn to me as a person.

I told you....... I made some mistakes......., I was not kidding

I thought

**Who would want to hear from me?**
**I was nothing to write home about**
**I grew up in foster homes**
**I got married**
**I got divorce**
**I got remarried**
**I had kids, grandkids**

WOW what would I have to say?

The mind of a 43 year old........

My doubting feelings finally were defeated by my overwhelming feelings that I was born to write.

Writing meant more to me......than just writing.

I AM PERFECTLY AND WONDERFULLY MADE AND POWERFUL BEYOND MEASURE!

_______________________________________________

(Don't forget to write down the above statement about you!)

Writing meant……. I was becoming the person who I was born to become.

If the words of my book just help one person complete and release their purpose to the world or if I die tomorrow…..

You are holding my purpose today. MY BOOK!

My book is my personal mark on this earth….

**Danyelle L Dickson was here**….

**YOU ARE STILL HERE ……..**

Your purpose is equally as important as my book………. so accomplish what you started please.

What will be your mark?
What legacy will you leave?
Who will know…… you were here?

I don't want you to miss out……..

Completing your purpose will unlock the door to your **real life**…….. and the possibilities are endless

Now….. I cannot tell you to do something for me……. without me telling you how to do it.

I LOVE YOU TOOOOOO……..MUCH FOR THAT.

I AM PERFECTLY AND WONDERFULLY MADE AND POWERFUL BEYOND MEASURE!

___

(Don't forget to write down the above statement about you!)

I've enclosed tools, keys, lessons, and quotes in my book designed to show you how to start loving you.

I've positioned positive words everywhere in my book...... to show you how to work on and possibly complete your purpose before you finish the final page.

More important than the words in my book........ I need you to make up in your mind that you believe the words and finally finish **what you started.**

This book is going to give you **some tools** that will require you to do the following:

1. You must......Love you
2. You must......Forgive yourself
3. You must......Forgive others
4. You must......Work on your purpose daily.
5. You must......Share love with other people around you

The various steps and lessons contained in this book coupled with your belief....hopefully will lead you to your real purpose in life.

**Remember to believe in yourself always.......**

Please learn from all of my mistakes listed throughout this book. My pain should not fall void anymore.

**DON'T BE SHOCKED!**

(Don't forget to write down the above statement about you!)

Its' weird when you are shown an idea, vision, or intuition to do something different with your life....... you will always initially doubt yourself.

It's natural to doubt.......if you can accomplish your purpose....BUT... ....I say to you......screaming to the top of my lungs.................. **YOU CAN DO IT**

Out of the billions of people in the world........ The vision was shown to you.

That's right.....YOU......

The person you see every day in the mirror still has something great to offer the world you live in.

I have to be honest once again........

Looking at yourself in the mirror can cause delays..........If you look at yourself long enough........

You will talk yourself right out of your own purpose

Don't look at yourself....... until you are ready to believe in your endless abilities........doubt can lead you to.....a dead in road of non-completion.

So.....stop looking......if your thinking does not line up with your new vision or purpose in life.

**Imagine with me for a moment!**

I think there should be a huge library built.

This library has just been named the largest library in the world by the Genius Book of World Records.

Imagine the largest library you have ever walked into....... then multiply that library image times 100

That's how big this library is. **HUGE**

This is a special people library........and for the record........this **isn't** a quiet library.

This library was built only to hold special **people** books.

All the books in this library....... represent all the people in the world who were ever born with a purpose

For the record that's everyone

There is a book for everyone in the world located in this special library. EVERYONE

The book title is simply your name (**yes you're in this library to**) and the name everyone who was ever given a vison, dream, or purpose to full-fill before they died.

This library would have sections like every other library......but these sections would separate the books by the title of the person's purpose.

(Don't forget to write down the above statement about you!)

So all the Doctor's would have a section,
All the Presidents would have a section.
All the Business Owners would have a section
All the Workers would have a section
All the Authors would have a section….You get my drift

This is not a quiet library because **every time** you or anybody else……stop or quit working towards completing something they started.

**BAM!**

There would be a person on the loud speaker in the library or better yet in your personal ear.

The voice is sort a like…… the voice you hear when you are shopping in stores……

You know the voice telling you about the store's specials.

The voice that says…….clean up on aisle 9…..we all heard that same voice from time to time.

That same pleasant voice…… you would hear in your ear…… if you had the same purpose as the person who just stopped working on their purpose.

**I really need you to get this……FOCUS**

(Don't forget to write down the above statement about you!)

In the world of earplugs and blue tooth's......Imagine you were connected by Bluetooth throughout your day...... every day...... to all the persons that had the same purpose as you to complete.

Every time they stopped working towards completing their purpose..... you would hear a small 10 second commercial......

**Danyelle has stopped her purpose again**, or **Danyelle is off the path from completing her goal again**.

I used my name on purpose........because from this day forward **you will never stop** doing what you were born to do

But imagine....... no matter where you are in the world....... you would be notified and hear that same recording instantly.......every time someone stopped working towards their purpose.

**Would that be motivation or what?**

For instance......The earphones would only be in the ears of certain people who had the same purpose titles.

Doctors, Lawyers, Actors, etc...Like me writing this book there are millions of authors right?

Well my earphones would be connected to all the other Authors who had a desire to write and publish a book before they die.

We are connected........ But I think you are especially connected to the people who have the same purpose as you.

(Don't forget to write down the above statement about you!)

Well...... NOW...... I have instantly connected you by Bluetooth to everyone who has the same purpose as you in this world.

I told you earlier if you have a vision and don't act on it....... someone else will bring it to pass.

**YOU CAN BET ON THAT**

1. Some people who hear this recording will get discouraged
2. Some people will even stop working towards their own purpose,
3. Some people would become energized to keep pushing towards their personal purpose so they **wouldn't** to hear their name over the loud speaker.

What I'm trying to convey in this section....... Is.........

**NEVER STOP WORKING TOWARDS YOUR PURPOSE OR YOUR GOAL** because even through there is no loud speaker or Bluetooth in your ear.......**This world needs you and your completed purpose**.

**Let's Talk for a moment..........**

**I know!**

You give soooooooooo much.....to sooooooooo many people, your job, your family, your mate, your friends, your boss and your co-workers.

I AM PERFECTLY AND WONDERFULLY MADE AND POWERFUL BEYOND MEASURE!

---

(Don't forget to write down the above statement about you!)

I know there are some days that you are just sooooooooo physically and mentally drained....... you feel you can't do anything else.

I know because I have been there ..... But that's when........ I need you to work towards your purpose anyway.......

Let the last thing you work on when you are tired be about you for once.

Even if you only have 10 minutes left before you go to sleep... to reflect, clear your mind and write out a to-do-list to complete tomorrow.

**THERE IS AN ANNOINTING in pushing past your exhaustion feelings....some of your greatest ideas will be revealed to you during those times.**

Just know....... we all get multiple opportunities to complete our purpose...... but.......
I believe if you **<u>don't</u>** finally complete your purpose......... then someone else will.

Haven't you been out somewhere.... it could have been sitting around the office or maybe at a dinner party and remember hearing the older gentleman or woman saying......

I thought of that idea years go. You instantly thought Yea right!

They were telling the truth.

(Don't forget to write down the above statement about you!)

Bottom line is....... **a thought not acted upon......** just lets the universe know......that someone.......somewhere........needs that idea.

Believe me when I tell you.....

When there **is a need** someone will **appear with the courage** and the skill set to fulfill that need.

People all over the world....... or maybe the people in your community need your purpose to be completed.

So, this is book is an example of me **not** focusing of myself long enough to write to write this book you.

Now the world is waiting for your completed purpose to be shared with them......

**Take a walk with me!**

Have you ever tried to explain or even recommend a book and the first thing that comes out of your mouth.....is the part you thought...... was the best part of the entire book?

But really when examine your words.........Your explanation wasn't the best part of the entire book.... it's really the part that related the most to you or your current situation.

You know the part of the book that moved you, agreed with you, or maybe just confirmed how you were feeling at the time.

It's that part of the book that when you're explaining to someone else your voice changes (goes a little higher pitched) and the person you are telling about that part can hear the excitement in your voice.

That feeling.... that excitement feeling....... I'm describing right now....... really goes beyond just reading books, it transcends to a lot of things in our lives.

You could be telling someone about a restaurant with exceptional food, a good movie, a speech, or even a sermon, and you for whatever reason find a phase, a point conveyed that you felt was just for you.

You love that part so much you immediately had to.... re-twit, blog it, Facebook it or send out in an email message.

That's the feeling that I'm talking about.....

And for the record...I know without a shadow of a doubt....that part...... you were speaking about (that made your voice go higher when explaining it) truly was for you.

It doesn't matter how many people saw or read the same thing you were explaining.

**<u>If you took notice then that part was just for you.</u>**

You see....... I believe that we are lead to books, movies, sermons, speeches, pictures, quotes, television shows, and even people...... in an effort to get us to complete what we started.....in our life.

(Don't forget to write down the above statement about you!)

There is always a power……. behind our power…… pushing us to our destiny…or trying to push some of you.

In everything we as a people will ever read, hear or see……we **all** have the same opportunity to get **that part** that relates to only us.

That's deep huh?

**But keep reading I'll explain**.

It's not that we will have the same feelings……. about the same part…… but….we all have the same opportunity to get a feeling,

We all get to take away…… some feeling…..about everything we will ever experience as we go through in life.

EVERYTHING

In order to reach completing your purpose…… you have to become a person that **will not** allow anything that is brought to you…… to pass you by…..without getting **something good** out of it.

**Everything** that is brought to you today and **everything** that you have gone through in the past…… is a direct result of your personal thoughts.
My desire is that you try to **always** find a way to **see good** in everything that crosses your path from this day forward.

I do mean **EVERYTHING**.

I AM PERFECTLY AND WONDERFULLY MADE AND POWERFUL BEYOND MEASURE!

---

(Don't forget to write down the above statement about you!)

I heard something somewhere and it read like this:

***"I NEVER FAIL,***

***I WIN***

***OR***

***I LEARN."***
***UNKOWN AUTHUR***

From this day forth.....please believe me....... and try live the above statement about everything that you encounter.

Believing and living that motto (seeing good in everything) will expedite you and ensure you will be allowed to finally complete your purpose. **Mark my words**

Some things........ As a matter of fact **all** things we will ever encounter......are God's way of getting us to look at our beautiful selves.

GOD wants you to notice how beautiful you really are
GOD wants you to notice how strong you really are
GOD wants you to notice how forgiving you really are
GOD wants you to notice how caring you really are.

Look at you.

I AM PERFECTLY AND WONDERFULLY MADE AND POWERFUL BEYOND MEASURE!

______________________________________________

(Don't forget to write down the above statement about you!)

**Do you feel that your life lessons have made you a better person?**

1. **You would have never known** how smart you were...... if you were never asked a question you thought you didn't know the answer to
2. **You would have never known** how strong you were....... if you never had to carry the weight of something super heavy
3. **You would have never** learned to forgive others........unless something was done to you that required forgiveness.
4. **You would have never** learned how to lead....... until you simply got tired of following others
5. **You would have never** learned how to Love........unless you experienced some form of hate.

SO FACE IT........ NO MATTER WHAT YOU HAVE GONE THROUGH IN YOUR LIFE

**YOUR LIFE EXPERIENCES HAVE MADE YOU A BETTER PERSON.**

**Keep walking with me...................we are just getting started.**

You are **what you** think and **what you** say about you!

With an astounding emphasizes on **you really are**......WHAT **YOU** THINK..... AND WHAT **YOU** SAY ABOUT YOU!

**ONLY YOU!**

The beauty of your life journey is.....You can start working on completing your purpose at any time. **It's never too late.**

(Don't forget to write down the above statement about you!)

Think about it.... no-one else knows.....you are reading this book right......

Well nobody has to know......you are working towards completing your purpose.

**HUSH IS THE WORD**..........until **you are ready** to present your purpose to the world.

Since I'm keeping your purpose secret.....Can you do somethings for me?

1. I want you to remember the lessons....I placed in this book up until this point.
2. I want you to... complete all the steps at the end of this book,
3. I want you to.... be committed to completing your 21 day steps, repeating the sayings daily as instructed,
4. I want you to.....Go back to the part of my book that relates the most to you the moment you get discouraged
5. I want you to NEVER tell people what you are working on until you are ready for their responses

There is an anointing in doing things out of public sight. What people don't know won't hurt you .......and....You can always feel GOOD about you.

I know you need something good to happen to you for once.

We all yearn to receive something good..... it's natural (**you are not alone**).

This book I hope will be viewed as an example of good.........

(Don't forget to write down the above statement about you!)

I'm transferring my good to you right now if you are reading my book.

For some of you it's been a while since you have been given something good or even felt good about your current situation and it's ok.

**But aren't you ready to feel good?**

Our minds are the single handed most powerful creature on this plant.

Your mind is more powerful than the biggest Lion, the most powerful Bear, and the largest Python in the world.

I chose those 3 animals for a reason.

**FOCUS.........I need you to think**

**The Lion...... what is the LION known for?**

1. The King of the Jungle
2. His powerful jaws
3. His distinct roar.

Some experts say the sound of a Lion's roar is something to hear. Some believe there is nothing like it on our planet.

So let's look at your mind and compare it to the Lions roar.

1. The Lion is known for his sound and I promise.... you are known for your sound. (**your words**)

I AM PERFECTLY AND WONDERFULLY MADE AND POWERFUL BEYOND MEASURE!

(Don't forget to write down the above statement about you!)

2. What are you allowing to come out of your powerful jaws? (**your mouth**)
3. What are you allowing to cross your powerful mind? (**your thoughts**)

**I believe…… your spoken words…… are your thoughts reality…. it just that simple.**

Think about it…….a Lion can command order by his sound………. insight fear just by the length of his sound……… ask animals to stand at attention or flee………..all by his sound?

You have the very same power and ability as the Lion.

1. Use your mind and your words to command negative thoughts and people to flee from your presence
2. Use your mind to command the world to recognize your purpose finally
3. Use your mind and thoughts to command a change in your life for the better
4. Use your mind to command your thoughts to forgive
5. Use your mind to command your words and thoughts to Love unconditionally.

When you truly unlock and operate daily on a positive plane…..

The most powerful thing that you will ever process, "YOUR MIND", will unlock and reveal your purpose by itself.

**I can't hold it anymore…… all of us have one common purpose that is true for us all.**

I AM PERFECTLY AND WONDERFULLY MADE AND POWERFUL BEYOND MEASURE!

______________________________________________

(Don't forget to write down the above statement about you!)

Our common purpose is to use our mind and thoughts to reveal who we really are to the world.

**GOOD……. POWERFUL……., LOVING……..,GIVING…….. AND A FORGIVING PEOPLE.**

When you really start understand and use your mind for positive things only……………….you will realize that your mind is stronger than a LION.

When you unlock and feed your mind positive thoughts daily (really every second of the day) then you will be on the right road to completing your purpose and gifted the ability to change the world around you.

**The Bear, What is the Bear known for?**

1. His size
2. His claws
3. His bear hug

**Work with me I'm going somewhere.**

Think about how we compare to a bear.

1. To a bear….. we are smaller in size
2. To an ant, cat, dog, or even a chicken…..**we are just as tall as a bear to them**
3. The bear has a great diet….the Bears eat berries, fish, plants, but even though his diet may seem small to us…….. standing on his hind legs some…..bears can stand 10 feet tall

(Don't forget to write down the above statement about you!)

This comparison.....is a little far-fetched.....but stay with me

What I'm trying to get you understand ....**We have to use our diet, our legs, and our hugs for good.**

What are you putting into your body that carries the most powerful thing on this planet (**your mind**)?

If you carry the most precious thing to date **(your mind)**............ then why you are not considering what you are putting into your body?

This is not a section designed to promote diets or even promote a certain body style or type is better..... Because it's not

We were all made beautiful and we are all powerful no matter what size we happen to be.

Simply put......we have to take care of the physical carrier of our mind. That's all.

If you are suffering from any disease........you have the power to ask your body to line up with healing........and guess what your body will.

Some of you are doing tooooooo much..........learn how to rest like the bear.

I'm not saying hibernate but I am saying.............learn how to rest your body, soul, and mind sometimes.

I AM PERFECTLY AND WONDERFULLY MADE AND POWERFUL BEYOND MEASURE!

______________________________________________

(Don't forget to write down the above statement about you!)

**NEWS FLASH.........Your body needs rest.**

What if I told you.........your body heals best when you are asleep?

When you think of healing before you go to bed.......... lie down with healing on your mind then the cells of your body...... will line up with other healing cells....BAM...your body is healing itself........

This process only works if you don't allow doubt to come in. (which generally happens when we are awake)

**Remember not medical advice in anyway just my opinion, my story, my truth.**

This section is not designed to offer healing practices

I am just simply pointing out......

1. You have the power over your own body,
2. You have the power to decide what you put in your body, a
3. You have the power to decide what diagnosis you accept about your own body.

There will come a time or two.......where you will have to stand on your hind legs...... grab the negative thought or thing that is in front of you.......... and squeeze the life out of it.

If you are living and operating based on the negative images of your past then you will have to do this drill more than others.

(Don't forget to write down the above statement about you!)

One thing is true.....the past is the past...... you must squeeze the negative images and thoughts out of your past and begin to see the positive aspects of your past.

You **were not** born to bow down to anything negative on this earth.

Use your bear arms and wrap your mind and thoughts around positive images only.

Everything on this earth is supposed to serve and bow down to you.

Use your hind legs now........to rise above your current circumstance, use your massive arms to crush every negative thought or thing that evades your space.

If the negative thing is a person in your past or present then use your arms and reach out to them give them................ **a hug good bye**.

Be sure when you are hugging them...... you are not squeezing the life out of them either.

We are a civilized people right........we just don't go around crushing humans.

**I had to put that in there because I want you to get this analogy.**

Sometimes all you **will ever** have to do to be successful is **hug** a person goodbye.

But you need them to live in your mind and your heart......... even if they are physically dead to complete this process.

I AM PERFECTLY AND WONDERFULLY MADE AND POWERFUL BEYOND MEASURE!

(Don't forget to write down the above statement about you!)

It's time for you to forgive the people who may be dead in your life both physically and emotionally whether it was their choice or yours.

They are no longer present in the physical or emotional realm so just........

**Love them, thank them, and let them go in your mind and in your heart.**

**This is an important step. I promise**

You need to wish positive things happen to them even for the negative people who may have hurt you in the past.

**Forgiving and letting people go is an important step to unlocking and utilizing the power you have.** Repeat yes....

Now.......that hug you just read about..... does not have to be in person, it could be a hug by email, or a hug by phone or even a hug by thought.

Whatever way you let them go finally really is up to you.... But I need you to squeeze the negative thoughts you have about that person out of your mind and heart right now.

MAN......this is a vital necessary exercise to remain on the right road to completing your purpose

**Back to my analogy.......(Fragment I know)**

**The Python, What is the Python known for?**

(Don't forget to write down the above statement about you!)

The python his known for his massive size.......his ability to crush and swallow animals that are much much larger than he is

For this analogy......I want you imagine a Python swallowing an alligator.

Believe or not I saw that very same imagine on a video I was watching.

**How does a Python compare to you?**

The Python is not scared to swallow something larger then him...I want you to think about your ability to take in much more information and positive affirmations then your body size can handle.

In a world where you have access to negativity at all times you have to stay over full on positive things instead of negative things.

In order for you to remain on the right road and being granted the ability to complete your purpose before you die.....

You have to feed your mind, body and soul with positive personal development as much as possible.

Throughout the day you need to look at a positive video or quote at your every break if you are working, **after every negative** thought, meeting, or phone call.

1. I need you to keep a positive saying around your desk (visible at all times)

I AM PERFECTLY AND WONDERFULLY MADE AND POWERFUL BEYOND MEASURE!

______________________________________________

(Don't forget to write down the above statement about you!)

2. I need you to have ready ........a positive text message or a positive email in the drafts section of your email or on your cell phone.
3. It doesn't matter where you to put your positive messages or scriptures... what matters is......you can see positivity at any time you need to see it.

A Python can eat a meal so big that he may not need another meal for weeks or even months.

You are different ....you need to have access to positive images, videos, quotes, every minute.... really every second of the day because you are surrounded by negativity on all sides.

You cannot eat the breakfast in the morning (YOUR MORNING MEDIATION) but skip lunch (THE POSITIVE VIDEO) then have dinner (YOUR NIGHT MEDITATION).

You are **<u>not full</u>** to capacity and you are subject to being weak when a negative thought comes your way or life hits you in the gut.

**<u>Remember the Python doesn't skip a meal until he is completely filled up.</u>**

Once the Python eats a large meal..... He is just able to lie around and wait for his food to digest.

You are very different in this matter also. You are not just lying around digesting your positive meal.

(Don't forget to write down the above statement about you!)

How many times have you been full to capacity but still had to go back to work....... or go back to getting things done.

You are surrounded by negativity from all sides...... so you need to eat positive thoughts and words constantly.

**Repeat yes......did you get why?**

I promise if you stay full on positive images and thoughts....... when negativity shows up.......you can replace those negative feelings with positive feelings more quickly.

**I hope you got the above lessons and just in case you had enough and stop reading right now.....remember**

This book is dedicated to feed your mind good thoughts and speak positive words into your life.

I pray by the end of this book.........you find that part of my book that you can speak about **(in that higher tone)** when telling or sharing a part of my book with someone you love.

More importantly and the real reason I wrote this book is to tell you......

Your ready............

My TRUE feelings behind this book and how I feel about you (my reader),

Before you keep reading: **JUST KNOW**

---

(Don't forget to write down the above statement about you!)

***YOU ARE LOVED TODAY***

***YOU ARE NEEDED TODAY***

***THE WORLD AND I HAVE BEEN PATIENTLY WAITING***

***FOR YOU TO***

***COMPLETE YOUR PURPOSE***

***SO JUST DO IT!***

**"IF I COULD GIVE YOU ONE THING IN LIFE, I WOULD GIVE YOU THE ABILTY TO SEE YOURSELF THROUGH MY EYES, ONLY THEN WOULD YOUR REALIZE HOW SPECIAL YOU ARE TO ME"**
**UNKNOWN AUTHOR**

It may be hard to believe that a perfect stranger loves you.

Well it's true the bible teaches me to "***owe no-man anything but to love one another***". Roman 13:8 KJV Copyright 1989 Thomas Nelson Inc. Printed in USA

(Don't forget to write down the above statement about you!)

So first off ..............I DO LOVE YOU

Second.....I really do need you to complete your purpose so you can help others around you and contribute to the world we live in.

The world we live in needs us all to do what we were born to do.......

I believe without a shadow of doubt **our world would change for the better**

My desire for you is that you finally see.......**you** have the power to change the world **you** live in.

Once you unlock and start to utilize your positive personal power for good.......the way you view the world as a whole....... will change right before your very eyes.

To start to unlock your purpose you must first acknowledge the fact

1. There is nothing you cannot accomplish......... if you put your mind to it.

Not the first time you heard that saying right.......but this is the first time you will start to believe and live that saying.

Now let's talk about the purpose that you will be given the opportunity to accomplish before you die.

I think you still have something to accomplish...something that will serve or help people all over the world or maybe just in your community.

I AM PERFECTLY AND WONDERFULLY MADE AND POWERFUL BEYOND MEASURE!

______________________________________________________________

(Don't forget to write down the above statement about you!)

Think about how many billions of people can be helped if just 2 million people would finally do what they were born to do.

So if I'm making this statement.......I must think that out of billions of people I don't believe that 2 million people are doing what they were born to do.

**Deep huh?**

You heard of the saying you are five people away from of a famous person or you are one idea away from being a millionaire.

Well think about this......

If millions of people start accomplishing their birth-given purposes and helping people all over the world.......***What would our world look like?***

My other desire is that some part, any part of this book will propel you to work and complete your purpose with speed because no one knows how many days we have left.

I always heard the saying "**tomorrow is not promise**" this is a truth that none of us can change.

I wrote this book to YOU because I SEE YOU as a part of my family and I truly want the best for you.

I want to share something with you right here and right now.

I AM PERFECTLY AND WONDERFULLY MADE AND POWERFUL BEYOND MEASURE!

---

(Don't forget to write down the above statement about you!)

**I BELIEVE** we are family no matter what color, sex, or religious beliefs….you have.

**YOU ARE MY FAMILY**…. and since I consider you my family…… it's only natural for me to share with you the very real fact……. we are connected.

**I BELIEVE** the very reason I was born was:

1. **To Write**
2. **To Encourage**
3. **To Motivate**
4. **To Drive**
5. **To Love**
6. **To propel** my family members including YOU to the next level in their lives…..

**Have to be honest with you right here once again.**

I did not always know what my purpose was or even operate in my purpose when I was younger.

Have to admit….. I made a lot of dumb mistakes in life by not adhering to the visons that were shown to me and about me.

**Being perfectly honest,**

I **did not** always see good in everything that was brought to me and I **would not** see good in everything that happen to me in my life.

**Being completely honest,**

---

(Don't forget to write down the above statement about you!)

I did not always make the right choices or even good choices for that matter, and that's why......... I'm so very thankful I **did not** die prior to me writing this book to you.

Family, I need you to know you are being granted a gift every day you wake up.

Each new day means you still have a **new opportunity** to do what you were born to do.

This book is literally an example of what you can do with a new day.

So let's go to work!

**"THE GREATEST DANGER FOR MOST OF US IS NOT THAT OUR AIM IS TOO HIGH AND WE MISS IT, "BUT THAT IT IS TOO LOW AND WE REACH IT" MICHELANGELE**

**Back to my book for a moment....**

If you have not already figured out why writing this book to you was life to me then know..........

I wrote this book because I wanted my long delayed purpose of being an Bestselling Author to be fulfilled.

All the words contain in this book are truly what I feel about each and every one of you (my readers).

(Don't forget to write down the above statement about you!)

If this book is read long after I die...... I wanted my book to be dedicated to my motto

## "ALWAYS *POSITIVE AND NEVER NEGATIVE*"

I mean all the words printed in this book from the bottom of my heart.

The words of this book mean more to me then you will ever know.

I did not die before this book was written which further confirms that you still have time to do what you were born to do.

With all the negatively in the world today,

I (little old me) got the opportunity to spread positivity, through the pages of my book,

I got the opportunity to say to you..... I love you and need you......... to everyone who will ever get to this part of my book.

I have to get off this part...... because Man........tears are rolling down my face even writing those words.

Please don't just read through this book fast...... I want you to read, pondered, imagine, understand, and believe the words you are reading;

I AM PERFECTLY AND WONDERFULLY MADE AND POWERFUL BEYOND MEASURE!

---

(Don't forget to write down the above statement about you!)

**<u>THIS IS WHAT I NEED FROM YOU (MY READERS)</u>**

1. I need you to believe all the words you have read up until this point of the book
2. I need you to believe all of the positive words you see throughout this entire book are true about you.
3. I need you to believe you are loved and your purpose is needed in this world we share.

I want you to promise me.....to say positive words about yourself every day for 21 days and then start over again.....if you have to.

I need you to say positive words until you believe the words and until you complete your purpose.

One factor to unlocking your purpose and reaching your goals is to **know whatever you think about ....is what will be in your life.**

**So, if <u>you think positive</u>** and **<u>speak positive</u>** then **<u>your life</u>** will become **<u>positive</u>**.

The opposite is true, **<u>BUT</u>**

I will **<u>never</u>** give any energy to anything negative...... so you just have to know....

If you think negative then your life will become negative. **That's it that's all.**

**<u>Let's be real right here!</u>**

I AM PERFECTLY AND WONDERFULLY MADE AND POWERFUL BEYOND MEASURE!

---

(Don't forget to write down the above statement about you!)

**I have to be honest again**,

You **are not** going to have 21 consecutive days where you **are not** going to hear something negative about you.......or.......... even have 21 consecutive days that something negative will not creep into your own mind about you.

**That's impossible......BUT**

The one thing that will separate you from the rest of people in this world......is what you do with that negative thought.

Are you going to cast it down immediately?

OR

Are you going to allow that negative thought to root in your mind, heart and soul?

When a negative thought creeps in........however it comes.......you must learn how to use negative thoughts to your advantage.

**Let me show you how....**

You can do one of the exercises you read thus far.....they work...but here is another way........ I want you to try.

For 21 days whenever negative thoughts happen...... the first thing I want you to instantly realize is.....................it happens to all of us...

**Don't beat yourself up.**

When negative things show up in whatever forms.......**I want you to just be thankful,**

Just being thankful for the negative thought.....will lead you to being able to change that negative thought to a positive thought faster......

The faster you can complete this exchange (changing negative thoughts to positive thoughts) is the faster you will be allowed to go back to working on completing your purpose

The moment you master this exercise you will somehow heighten your awareness to the GREAT power you have trapped inside of you.

You will finally learn once and for all, that circumstance (that negative thought) only made you a stronger better person in the end.

Don't be like the people who stay stuck in negative images and circumstances ... separate yourself.

Separation and completion of your purpose comes when you learn to cast down every negative thought that comes in or to you......... and replace it with a positive thoughts or images.

If you ever want to accomplish and complete your purpose you have to master that skill.

**REPEAT....YES........I HOPE YOU GOT THAT POINT**

I AM PERFECTLY AND WONDERFULLY MADE AND POWERFUL BEYOND MEASURE!

______________________________________________

(Don't forget to write down the above statement about you!)

Notice……..

I did not say that negative thoughts will not appear……

They will, what I am trying to say is…….

The opposite…… of negative…..is positive….

So **every time** a negative thought creeps in…….. I want you to replace it with a positive thought. **EVERY TIME**

If you don't master this skill and do this exercise of replacing good with bad then your purpose will be always be delayed and for some of you unfortunately your purpose will never happen.

NEVER

Sadly some people in life have never spoken positive things over themselves.

I need you to do an exercise for me so I can make sure that you are speaking positive things about you.

Write down all the good and positive things you can think about the wonderful you.

You better write down something right here**…..I'm not playing**

1. I am ______________________________
2. I am ______________________________
3. I am ______________________________

I AM PERFECTLY AND WONDERFULLY MADE AND POWERFUL BEYOND MEASURE!
___________________________________________

(Don't forget to write down the above statement about you!)

4. I am ___________________________________
5. I am ___________________________________

You have to be a person who can say positive things about yourself just in case no one else ever does.

I need you to become a person who starts your day and end your nights with positive words about you.

The words contained in this book are the TRUTH about who you really are .......

Its time you started to believe.........in you.

This book is GOD'S infinite way to get a message to you.

A message that you ask for........and because you are loved so much.......

Your request for help was granted

You're reading this book right?

If you're reading this book......**YOU** and **ONLY YOU** have the opportunity to change your life.....

**That statement is not hype......... but keep reading you will understand shortly.**

If you are reading this book there is something that you **YOUR SELF** have not accomplished yet point blank period.

I AM PERFECTLY AND WONDERFULLY MADE AND POWERFUL BEYOND MEASURE!

______________________________________________

(Don't forget to write down the above statement about you!)

To unlock your goal or purpose was the reason for this book and the sole reason why you are still living for that matter.

SO from the gate..... Be thankful you have not accomplished what you think you should have accomplished before now.

Sometimes an **un-accomplished goal** is a good thing.

I know in the world of deadlines you think you should be further along in your life.

Well I'm telling you to STOP beating yourself up and start questioning and exploring what else you would like to accomplish before you die.

I promise there is something new you still have to do.

Oh that rhymes smile.......

***"THERE IS SOMETHING NEW....***
***YOU STILL HAVE TO DO"***

**I'm sorry...... I do need you to focus right now......BUT**

I told you writing to you unlocked so many good things for me......

Soon as I typed that statement something in my spirit brought me overwhelming joy.

I AM PERFECTLY AND WONDERFULLY MADE AND POWERFUL BEYOND MEASURE!

---

(Don't forget to write down the above statement about you!)

That very statement just may be the title of my next book or maybe my world speaking tour title....that leads millions of people all over the world to acknowledge the gift of life and not the curse of their past.

Repeat .........on purpose.

## *"THERE IS SOMETHING NEW...*
## *YOU STILL HAVE TO DO"*

**Back to you!**

If you have not reached your personal purpose or goal before now you may have **unconsciously** or more dangerous **consciously** took on the image of what people have said about you.

So many of us **falsely** feel that we are:

Who our bank account says we are
Who our job says we are
Who our marriage says we are,
Who being single says we are,
Who our past says we are,
Who our incomplete purpose says we are
Who our economic status says we are,
Who our religious beliefs says we are

**The list goes on and on.........**

The most dangerous thought of everything listed above is........

---

(Don't forget to write down the above statement about you!)

The image of **what you personally believe about yourself.**

It's very easy to change people's perception or better yet....it's very easy to fool people about who you really are deep down inside.

There are so many un-happy women and even more un-happy men on jobs and in relationships they absolutely hate but they put on a front every day of their lives.

Men lead meetings everyday........He so good at putting on a front........all his co-workers think he absolutely loves his job............ but the reality is he hates his job and doesn't even support the vision of the company.

We have been programmed to put on a front.

Everybody has now been programmed to lie about who they really are as a person

**FRANKLY......I'm tired of it**

So many people are living a lie these days it's hard for me to keep up. People today are scared to show people who they really are.

It has somehow become dangerous to express your personal opinions and your personal truths about yourself.

**Weird Huh? (Fragment yes I know)**

1. I remember a time when you could level with someone without leveling them as a person.

(Don't forget to write down the above statement about you!)

2. I remember a time when you could agree to disagree(it was not that serious)
3. I remember a time when you were taught to love people even if you did not accept what the person was doing.

For this section……I want to focus on you……. and I'm telling you……. it's time to

**STOP LYING.**

I don't know what lie you are living…… but if your lie is contributing to or feeding you a false image or yourself……..then I have a problem it (the lie that is).

**The lie you're living does not hurt anybody but you!**

You only have one life to live so take **full advantage** of the time you have left.

**Why are you not living your life for you?**

I love you………. but I really need you to love yourself more.

**ALL OF YOURSELF**

**INCLUDING YOUR PAST SELF**

You have to think, write, and speak positive things about yourself at all times.

**Your mind has no space for negatively and no more time to loose.**

(Don't forget to write down the above statement about you!)

Every page I write.... I had to recognize that changing my mindset to positive always applied to me first.

You see it took me 33 years to accomplish a vision that was given to me at approximately 10 years old.

**The truth is........**

1. It took me 8 years after I told people I was going to write this book to actually sit down and write it.
2. Not writing and not doing what I was born to do lead me to have a slew of discouragement feelings (30 years' worth).

**I asked myself all the time!**

**Why did I tell people about my book that was not published?**

You see when you are given the vision of your purpose....... it's natural to want to share it with someone....... **Your excited right?**

However when you share your purpose and you don't keep on your task...... you will face a world win of mixed negative emotions.

**Let's talk about me for a moment!**

I told you....my negative feelings....always lead me to start asking myself questions.....

What was I thinking?..............Better yet what are they thinking?"

Danyelle why haven't you done what you were born to do?"

---

(Don't forget to write down the above statement about you!)

The moment you share your purpose with others all kind of emotions will cross your mind because they crossed mine.

The true gift was................ that I still had time to write and publish this book.

So does it matter if you have shared your purpose with someone and have not accomplished it yet?

**NO**

Use those un-fulfilled feelings not to beat yourself up(repeat yes) but to motivate yourself to get off your butt and start working on completing your purpose again.

**IT'S NOT TOO LATE**.....

If you're reading my book and have been paying attention while you're reading.......

Then you know my book should be a reflection that you still have time.

**Keep reading we are just getting to the best stuff!**

When you feel you have wasted time than know.......there is a sometimes there is a bigger plan that we cannot see at first.

Got to get deep again..... I believe

(Don't forget to write down the above statement about you!)

The pages of this book were spoken into existence before I was ever born.......

The pages you are reading were the pages that stuck out the most to me when I was writing.

I deleted several pages because I was not writing this book for me... ......I was writing this book to you.................. And only you

I made a vow never to give any of **my energy** to any negative thoughts or images effective January 1, 2015

When people were making New Year resolutions I was making a positive mind shift change for once in my life.

So since my book was published after my effective date this book is patterned after my new positive motto. I hope you join me.

**POSTIVE THOUGHTS ONLY ALLOWED!**

**NOT JUST FOR THE REST OF THIS BOOK**

**BUT I PRAY FOR THE REST OF YOUR LIFE**

So here it goes positively....

***YOU ARE PEFECTLY AND WONDERFULLY MADE AND POWERFUL BEYOND MEASURE.***

Now, I know just by me writing that statement something negative possibly popped into your head.

I AM PERFECTLY AND WONDERFULLY MADE AND POWERFUL BEYOND MEASURE!

---

(Don't forget to write down the above statement about you!)

**Did you instantly think?**

1. "**She cannot be writing about me**".
2. "**She cannot know what I'm going through right now**."
3. "**There is no way I am perfectly and wonderfully made and powerful beyond measure**".

My answers to all those questions are**:**

**I AM TALKING TO YOU**

I don't know what you are going through right now……. but……

I do know we all have to go through some difficult things to get us to realize how special we really are.

Believe me when I tell you I had to go through some things…… but as promise **always positive**……. **never negative** from this point on.

Family you have to realize that what you are going through or even went through in the past **didn't break you…… it didn't kill you.**

**YOU ARE LIVING…….. YOU ARE NOT DEAD**!

You are reading this book right?

I will **never** give power to your current situation.

I would simply prefer to **give power to WHO you are becoming?**

**I love the person you are becoming.**

I AM PERFECTLY AND WONDERFULLY MADE AND POWERFUL BEYOND MEASURE!

(Don't forget to write down the above statement about you!)

My desire for you just by reading *THE WORDS* throughout this whole book was designed for you to learn the importance of speaking positive words about you.

You're reading a book completely dedicated to introducing you....... to your beautiful self

***YOU ARE PEFECTLY AND WONDERFULLY MADE AND POWERFUL BEYOND MEASURE.***

You lead me.......you willed me......to personally designed and position positive words in and throughout this entire book.

That's how powerful you are.......I wrote about you (my reader)...... long before you pick up this book.

You see **I knew** the day would come that you would be lead to this book and **I knew** this book would contain something just for you.

Another key to unlocking your purpose is realizing "**you are whatever you say you are**".

Speaking positive about you is a necessary requirement to unlocking your purpose.

You bought this book and I don't believe you bought this book for nothing.

Once you learn to speak positive things about you and your situation daily......you will unlock your ability to change your reality at ANY TIME.

I know you heard of the peoples overnight success stories.

I feel those people simply unlocked their birth given ability to change their reality at any time.

Every one of us have that same power but ........you must learn to live for today and not live from the point of your past or your past mistakes.

**If you want to change your reality then do it.**

**Disclaimer: The change happens in an instant but sometimes your mind will not allow you to physically see the change in an instant ...........and it's ok.**

If you can't visualize the change right now then start acknowledging your new positive feelings of change.

Wake up and go to bed with an overwhelming feeling that your life is different and it will be different. I promise

Start living your life with the power you have
Knowing you control how you feel about anything that has ever happen to you
Knowing you have the power to feel any way you want to about everything that will ever happen to you in the future.

You know you are tired of carrying some of your past feelings.

**JUST...... LET THEM GO!**

(Don't forget to write down the above statement about you!)

You cannot change your past.....So why do you keep reliving something that happened years ago?

**It's only hurting you.**

Do you remember as a child falling down and getting a sore?

What I loved about the sore process is that every time I fell........

I got attention from my mom....... which I liked (we all do).........,
but when my sore healed.......

I only got a scab and I did not get the same attention as when it first happened.

My mom would say "**Danny don't ripe off that scab**". She told my scab meant my sore was healing.

Every once in a while I would ripe off the scab of my sore.

What would happen?

My sore even though it didn't just happen........would bleed again

I realized my **old sore** was bleeding again....... my **old sore** didn't hurt as much as it did when it first happened......... but it still bled.

This series I just explained is what happens to you when you rip the scab off of your past for whatever reason.

Some of you are stuck........literally lost in your past feelings ......

---

(Don't forget to write down the above statement about you!)

You ripped off the scab of your **old past** by telling your story again for sympathy and now you are looking at the new blood that **you caused**.

You ripped off the scab but never realized that this **new blood** and the pain is not the same as when it first happened.

Even though your sore (you) are bleeding (hurting) again.....

You **are not** the same person ..........you were when it first happened.

SO........**STOP RIPPING OFF YOUR SCABS.**

**THEY ARE HEALED...... LET THEM BE HEALED.**

You have the power to replace those hurt feelings....... with the feelings...... of a healed person.

**I have to say it again! I just have to!**

You have the power to replace those **hurt** feelings with the feelings of a **healed** person.

I wish I can change everything that has happened to you................ but I can't.....

So know I can offer you this thought.

**It is better for you to promote positive feelings then negative feelings from this day forward.**

I AM PERFECTLY AND WONDERFULLY MADE AND POWERFUL BEYOND MEASURE!

---

(Don't forget to write down the above statement about you!)

I'm many things............................ but I'm not foolish.

Until your faith catches up to the truth about whom you really are you are just going to have to take on my belief system

I told you this book is dedicated to speaking and declaring who you really are daily....... even if you can't believe the words right now.

I love you sooooooo much that all you have to do is keep reading.

**I'm sorry well NO I'm not sorry**

**You will simply have to read it and say it again.**

***"I AM PEFECTLY AND WONDERFULLY MADE AND POWERFUL BEYOND MEASURE".***

Here I go with one of my desires........smile

One of my desires is for you to KNOW that you are **those words** and have always been those words by the time you read the final chapter in my book.

Please learn to really believe those very words, start speaking those words about yourself, as well as others in your life.

So many people today share in victim stories but not enough people share in positive declarations and victory stories.

***Speak it once more but this time I want you to SHOUT it out***

(Don't forget to write down the above statement about you!)

***"I AM PEFECTLY AND WONDERFULLY MADE AND POWERFUL BEYOND MEASURE"***

1. Now that I have made you say it just by putting those words in this section.
2. I made you read it again by repeating those words in this section
3. I even made you SHOUT it

I purposely put those words as many times as I could in this section and you will see those very same words more than any other words contain in my book,

**WHY?**

Partly because I know how....... I feel about you........ BUT...... more importantly

I know how you possibly feel about yourself right now........ And your feelings might be so far from the true feelings **YOU ARE PERFECTLY AND WONDERFULLY MADE AND POWERFUL BEYOND MEASURE.**

**YOU will be ok ......**its time that you realize your worth and your worth **is not** determined by your current situation or your past mistakes.

It's time for you to realize........YOU ALREADY...... PAID THE COST IN FULL...... by still living and not giving up.

I AM PERFECTLY AND WONDERFULLY MADE AND POWERFUL BEYOND MEASURE!

______________________________________________

(Don't forget to write down the above statement about you!)

Put those same words ***"I AM PEFECTLY AND WONDERFULLY MADE AND POWERFUL BEYOND MEASURE"*** in a text to yourself, email yourself, write them on your calendar, place them in your wallet, your bathroom mirror, on your refrigerator, on the computer monitor, and anywhere you spend time looking at for any period of time.

It will be hard at first for you to maintain this mindset and imagine yourself as powerful beyond measure but you really are.

What would happen?

If you just made up in your mind that you will never quit speaking positive about yourself even when you don't hear it from anyone else.

To only focus on positive things and thoughts goes against the norm.....

I really need you to know that your personal words and your personal thoughts are far more powerful than the words you will read or see in my book.

I know when you finish my book it may go on a shelf somewhere or you may even give my book to someone else.

Let me be the first to say "giving my book away is not what I'm hoping for".

If you want to share my book then I want you to buy another book and give it to them.

I AM PERFECTLY AND WONDERFULLY MADE AND POWERFUL BEYOND MEASURE!

---

(Don't forget to write down the above statement about you!)

The words of my book were written to you (my reader) first.

If you think that someone else may need the words contained in my book...... then they need to buy their own book....Do not give up yours please.

I didn't write this book to be given away.

I know there will be times when you may go back to your old negative feelings and I just imagined you running back to the shelf pulling this book down and reading it again.

At least that's what I'm praying will happen.

I don't mind you adding this book to a book club or reading this book together as long as you remember as an individual that **I wrote this book to you specifically**.

**In my mother voice......**This book is personal.

This book requires you to write down things, imagine things, speak things, and even shout things about you and only you, **so this is not a book you can give away.**

It will defeat the very reason this book was birth in me.

Later I'm going to required you to say the 21 sayings, say them again for old time sake and write them down somewhere for the next 21 days.

(Don't forget to write down the above statement about you!)

To be honest I want you to start your day and end your night with positive words every day especially the next words.

**I AM PEFECTLY AND WONDERFULLY MADE AND POWERFUL BEYOND MEASURE**

Now that you said it...... there is only one more thing to do.....write those words down........and journal your journey.

I want you journal where you think you are today (whatever situation you are currently in) ......... and journal where you see yourself at the end of this book.

I know you will be closer to completing your purpose then you could have ever realized before reading my book.

Remember you are...... what and who....... you say you are.

You can accomplish anything that you set your mind and your feelings to.

The key is to never stop reaching toward your goals and to always keep your mind and feelings positive.

I'm not going to require you to go out and buy a journal because I said everything you need is already in you.

If I'm going to require you to do something for me......the least I can do is.....do something for you.

_______________________________________________

(Don't forget to write down the above statement about you!)

You bought my book....... and I told you my book was very....... very personal.

**You did not know why until now**

So we are going to journal your journey together in this very same book.

There will be spaces on the top of every page so you can write down the 21 day statements enclosed in this book.

The statement above (I AM PEFECTLY AND WONDERFULLY MADE AND POWERFUL BEYOND MEASURE) was printed on the top of every page because I wanted you to never forget that statement....EVER

**"I AM PEFECTLY AND WONDERFULLY MADE AND POWERFUL BEYOND MEASURE"**

Fill in the blanks below.

Write down

**I AM PERFECTLY AND WONDERFULLY MADE AND POWERFUL BEYOND MEASURE"**

I believe in that statement with my heart, mind, and soul: Yes _____
Print Name: _______________________________________________
Signature: _______________________________________________
Date: _______________________________________________

I AM PERFECTLY AND WONDERFULLY MADE AND POWERFUL BEYOND MEASURE!

---

(Don't forget to write down the above statement about you!)

I too believe that statement about you!

I sign my name under penalty of perjury....... I believe that very statement about all who read this book! Especially about you who just made that declaration.

"I believe it also..... So IT IS SETTLED"

You don't get the opportunity to take that statement back...... you wrote it and therefore you have just activated the positive power within you.

Yes: **X**
Print Name: DANYELLE DICKSON
Date: WHAT EVER DAY AND YEAR YOU ARE READING THIS BOOK
SIGNATURE:

Danyelle Dickson

---

Witness by: Danyelle Dickson
I too believe that statement about you!
"IT IS SETTLED"

We are all born with a purpose; your first purpose is to fall in love with yourself, then you're ready to contribute something good to this wonderful planet we share.

**<u>STOP!</u>**

Your purpose is not for you to question or even wonder.

(Don't forget to write down the above statement about you!)

**Do I have a purpose?**

**Yes you do........ We all do.**

Your purpose may be big ........or your purpose may be small....... however I can assure you.......... you do have a purpose.

**You MUST know with a certainty that you were born to accomplish something**.

**Stay with me.....Focus**

Please know,

I **will not** allow you to be like the millions of people who died without fulfilling the very thing they were born to do.

Your purpose may be an invention, a book, a company, idea, concept, slogan, movie, song, or maybe you just have to love, help, or bring joy to one single person or to everyone you meet from this day forward.

You see.... you and everyone you see.....all around the world were born to accomplish something and I believe it's always a good thing.

What you need to focus on most importantly right now..... Is.......

You are still breathing..... And you still have time...... to accomplish your purpose, your goal, your dream or your desire before you die.

**Forgive yourself right now.**

I AM PERFECTLY AND WONDERFULLY MADE AND POWERFUL BEYOND MEASURE!

______________________________________________

(Don't forget to write down the above statement about you!)

I (Your Name)____________________________, forgive myself for not accomplishing (purpose)______________________, before now,

I forgive myself for everything I have done in my past.

I forgive all the people who have done something to me

I truly forgive myself today.

From this day forward

I will never live in regret.

Today I live like my slate is wiped clean.

Today I live the rest of my life...... to accomplish the very reason I was born...... and I will not allow anyone or anything stop me.

**I FORGIVE MYSELF AND TODAY**

**I REMEMBER" I AM PERFECTLY AND WONDERFULLY MADE AND POWERFUL BEYOND MEASURE"**

______________________________________________

I believe in that statement with my heart, mind, and soul: Yes: _____
Print Name: ______________________________________
Signature: ________________________________________
Date: ____________________________________________

Danyelle Dickson

______________________________________________

I AM PERFECTLY AND WONDERFULLY MADE AND POWERFUL BEYOND MEASURE!

______________________________________________

(Don't forget to write down the above statement about you!)

Witness by: Danyelle Dickson
I too believe that statement about you!
"IT IS SETTLED"

**Stay with me!**

Another key to unlocking your purpose is….. **You must forgive yourself.**

No matter what YOU have to forgive yourself for.

Another vital key to completing your purpose is forgiving others no matter what is it they may need to be forgiven for.

**THIS is a must**.

You cannot truly love yourself or accomplish your purpose without being able to forgive.

You may not be there yet (ready to forgive) but I pray that you learn to.

I **need** you to not only forgive but love and wish them well for shaping you into the person you are **finally** becoming before you read the last page of my book.

What they did to you or what you did to someone else only proved how strong of a people we really are.

Think about it like this.

(Don't forget to write down the above statement about you!)

There is someone waiting for you to share your testimony on how you forgave, and how your life was transformed for the better just for completing that forgiving act.

There may be someone one out there scared to share their secret for fear of what people will think.

You can will……. that scared person into your life…. they will only need to hear your survival story for them to learn how to forgive themselves.

Disclaimer: **Only use your past story when it is helpful to someone else and publicly confirming forgiveness is necessary.**

From this point on
Don't share your past story for sympathy…. but share your past story for the **sole reason** of helping someone else learn how to forgive.

You will never believe anything positive about you if you will not forgive yourself once and for all.

It's kinda like me telling you the sky is red…. But when you look up all you see is blue. If you don't believe me the analogy will not work for you.

I can speak positive words into your life throughout my entire book and positive words are purposely woven throughout this entire book but I still need YOU to believe the words you see and read and forgive once in for all.

I AM PERFECTLY AND WONDERFULLY MADE AND POWERFUL BEYOND MEASURE!

---

(Don't forget to write down the above statement about you!)

There is a method to my book and if you finally want a change in your life for the better... you have to do your part.

I put positive words everywhere in this book.....mainly to speak to your sub-conscious mind.

But if you **<u>don't</u>** or **<u>won't</u>** forgive yourself then the words of my book will fall VOID.

You have wasted enough time reliving your past.....now it's time to use the rest of your time left wisely.

1. Time... WOW TIME.... I feel time is the greatest gift granted to us.
2. Time....Gives you time to accomplish whatever you what to accomplish......
3. Time....Gives you time to heal...,
4. Time....Gives you time to forgive.......
5. Time....Gives you time to love....
6. Time....Gives you time to contribute

**<u>I feel time is our greatest gift!</u>**

Forgive yourself and others and you are one step closer to being gifted the ability to complete your purpose.

You must decide to love yourself no matter what your current situation is
You must decide to love yourself no matter what life did to you in your past.

(Don't forget to write down the above statement about you!)

**I repeated this section on purpose**

**Keep reading and remember you are loved**

We all have something that we need to be forgiven for and we all have a person who we need to forgive.

It does not matter the reason.

**I'm telling you to drop it once and for all.**

UN-Forgiveness only hurts you..... **NO** I take that back.....un-forgiveness hurts us all because you will never reach your purpose if you do not forgive and we can never benefit from your completed purpose.

I told you...... I believe we all are connected .......

FORGIVENESS DOES NOT MEAN YOU FORGET...... BUT

WHAT IT MEANS IS THAT.................... YOU NO LONGER LIVE AS A VICTIM.

If you were lead to buy my book

I know that you are a person that should be proud of the person you are today.

WHY?

I AM PERFECTLY AND WONDERFULLY MADE AND POWERFUL BEYOND MEASURE!

(Don't forget to write down the above statement about you!)

Because you are a person that has endured so much in life and you are still standing

**YOU SHOULD BE PROUD……**

**NOW GO AFTER YOUR PURPOSE…..**

Your purpose could be one thing or multiple things.

When you truly accomplish what you are born to accomplish (loving yourself and sharing yourself with others) your true purpose will be revealed and always changes.

When you get to another level in life….. You will always have a greater audience to effect but the first thing is overcoming your current situation.

I spoke to your past so I just have to speak to your current situation.

**Let's look at the OVERCOMERS**

Think about all the television stars, movie stars, athletes, inventors, and singers that are changing the world, giving and helping millions of people because they have the money to help them.

Many of them speak about their humble beginnings but they first had to forgive themselves, forgive others, speak positive, and go to work.

They could not afford to stay stuck in their beginnings (their current situations).

I AM PERFECTLY AND WONDERFULLY MADE AND POWERFUL BEYOND MEASURE!

_______________________________________________

(Don't forget to write down the above statement about you!)

I told you in the beginning of this book......that changing your life would not be easy but very necessary.

WHY?

**BECAUSE I NEED YOU, and THE WORLD NEEDS YOU.........**

**Imagine with me for a moment!**

Think about the people who were born without limbs and touch millions of people because they were able to accomplish their goals without the body parts people thought they needed to accomplish that goal.

In my mind their process, their order of events happened like this....

I imagined this process for them and I believe this order is the same for all of us.

1. They first had to be born without all their limbs,
2. Overcome what people thought about them not having all their limbs.(LOVE THEMSELVES anyway)
3. Believe they can accomplish anything they want to accomplish with or without limbs,
4. Accept that they were born to do the very goal birthed in them,
5. And then just do it
6. Lastly after their purpose was fulfilled
7. Watch millions of people get touched (moved) just by them being ok with doing what they were born to do.

I AM PERFECTLY AND WONDERFULLY MADE AND POWERFUL BEYOND MEASURE!

_______________________________________________

(Don't forget to write down the above statement about you!)

It's that simple but you make it so hard.

If you are reading my book and have all your limbs think about these steps.

8. You first had to be born to your parents(LOVE THEM NO MATTER WHAT)
9. Overcome what people thought about you and your environment.(LOVE YOUR BEGINNINGS NO MATTER WHAT)
10. Believe that you can accomplish anything that you want to accomplish no matter how long it takes (LOVE TIME NO MATTER WHAT)
11. Accept that you were born to do the very goal birthed in you, (LOVE YOURSELF NO MATTER WHAT)
12. And then just do it (NO MATTER WHAT)
13. Lastly after your purpose was fulfilled watch millions of people get touched (moved) just by you being ok with you and doing what you were born to do. (LOVE PEOPLE NO MATTER WHAT)

We may have one thing or multiple things that we were born to do.

Your purpose may be tiny to someone else or your purpose may be huge to someone else.

I have to be honest family.....

To accomplish your personal purpose if you have not completed it before now...... it will seem HUGE to you.....and sometimes even seem very out of reach!

I AM PERFECTLY AND WONDERFULLY MADE AND POWERFUL BEYOND MEASURE!

---

(Don't forget to write down the above statement about you!)

Your purpose is really in reach……. but you may be allowing your mind…… to play tricks on you and believe it's not.

Accomplishing your personal purpose is **as close** or **as far** as you believe it is.

**You are that powerful.**

The beauty of this section is that you can change the distance required to complete your purpose at any time.

If you're reading right now and your purpose seems far away…

I dare you to believe me (everything you have read up to this point)…..

Then I want you to personally decide that the road to completing your purpose is very short.

That road….I promise if you don't doubt….. Instantly become shorter.

**So why haven't you not reached your purpose yet?**

I want to offer up just a thought of why you have not reached your goals yet.

**Remember it's just a thought**

Could it be?

1. You went through life and you started to believe what people said about you

(Don't forget to write down the above statement about you!)

2. What your background says about you
3. What your age says about you
4. What your past mistakes say about you
5. What your past failures say about you.

THOSE THE ABOVE STATEMENTS ARE A LIE!

YOU CAN HAVE WHATEVER YOU CAN BELIEVE

Another key to unlocking your purpose is you must realize that your situation does not define you as a person;

Your current situation **does not** define your ability to accomplish your purpose;

Your current situation **can't even** stop you from completing your purpose.

1. You are not what your current situation says you are.
2. Your current situation is only temporary.
3. Who you are becoming as a person is permanent.
4. You can have whatever you can believe.

Think about all the situations in your life that have come and gone but you are still here.

I want to teach you **not to** focus on or believe that you are your current situation.

I want to teach you to demand your current situation to know who you are in that situation!

(Don't forget to write down the above statement about you!)

**POWERFUL!**

Demand your current situation to know that IT (WHATEVER IT IS) **will not** break you,

Your situation **will not** defeat you,

One thing is true.....your situation **will not** change

UNTIL you speak that (IT) needs to change.

Today you can start to speak life over your current situation and today your situation will change. I promise

You really are...... powerful beyond measure.

You heard of the saying....... you can speak to a mountain and it will move.

Well it's true you can speak to your current situation and it will change.....

**Back to work.**

Your purpose was designed just for you.

Your purpose is patiently waiting on you and only you to complete the things necessary to bring it to pass.

I AM PERFECTLY AND WONDERFULLY MADE AND POWERFUL BEYOND MEASURE!

(Don't forget to write down the above statement about you!)

But you MUST realize the following first:

1. You were born with everything needed to fulfill your purpose, even if on the outside people feel you do not have the right tools.
2. You are still living so there is something you still must accomplish.
3. You must from this day forward stop believing people and believe in yourself and your ability to do whatever you want to do...... and more importantly what you were born to do.
4. You must give no more room to negativity in your life.
5. You must learn what it takes to bring your purpose to pass (research)!
6. You must see and feel yourself as already accomplishing your purpose
7. You must work towards your purpose or goal every day.
8. You must realize you don't need anyone to approve of your purpose...because it was given to you.

You see GOD loves you so much that HE granted you another day and another opportunity to get it right.

Every single day really every single second of the day is a gift from our creator, for some a gift from the universe, for me another day is a gift from Jesus, for other people it may be a gift from a higher power.

It really doesn't matter who or what you choose to believe in...... please believe me.... there are millions of people who did not get to see today. **Reality check**

Now I used the analogy.... time as a gift...... in the above section because who doesn't like to get GIFT?

---

(Don't forget to write down the above statement about you!)

You remember the feeling you got.......when you knew the gift had your name on it

It was just for you!

You couldn't wait to see what's inside.

Whether you got a gift as a child or adult everyone......loves to gets gifts.

Now once you opened the gift.... it may or may not have been what you wanted

But for this section only...............remember the excitement feelings you got when you received something that was just what you always wanted.

Here is my philosophy of gifts.

I believe new days we are given are true gifts......
I also believe YOU are a gift.
**You and only you are a gift to the world**

YOU are wrapped in the prettiest paper (your mind, body and soul) and you are just what the world needs,

Your completed purpose will be shipped special delivery to peoples address all over the world or possibly just help the people in your neighborhood

I AM PERFECTLY AND WONDERFULLY MADE AND POWERFUL BEYOND MEASURE!

---

(Don't forget to write down the above statement about you!)

I hope your purpose.....the thing you want to complete before you die......is going to meet the needs of a verified market audience (people).

Research the supply and demand model. That was free

Think about it this way........

The world had to wait for you to complete your purpose

Just as we had to wait to get our gift for our birthday or maybe on a special occasion

**Good things come to those who wait right?**

Your time could be now.....If you want it to be

I pray your time is now but it's totally up to you.

**Keep reading!**

It may take a while for you to believe that analogy (you being a gift), so let's just agree on the following:

1. Each and every day that you wake up a higher power allows you another day to get it right,
2. Each and every day that you wake up a higher power allows you another opportunity to right wrongs,
3. Each and every day that you wake up a higher power allows you another opportunity to grow, inspire, and change for the better

(Don't forget to write down the above statement about you!)

Family......If you can only see every day...... as a day given to you....... as a day that allows you to do better than you did yesterday....... That's a huge mindset shift....

**Repeat for a reason...... GET THIS PLEASE**

More than you believing each day are new gifts .....What would happen if you start to enjoy your days for nothing more than just being grateful to be alive......

MAN....... that's when the magic starts.

The moment you learn to be grateful is when you receive another key to unlocking your purpose.

Being grateful about life finally will unlock your deep rooted personal positive power and grant you the ability to make the rest of your days whatever you want them to be.

Imagine a day that you created, you commanded, you allowed into being.

How powerful is that?

When you finally realize that you have the opportunity to be a gift to everyone you will ever meet,

1. Realize you are a gift wrapped up with the prettiest bow people ever seen (your positive words)
2. Realize people are waiting for their gift to be delivered to them (your completed purpose)
3. Realize time is the only thing you cannot get back.

I AM PERFECTLY AND WONDERFULLY MADE AND POWERFUL BEYOND MEASURE!

______________________________________________

(Don't forget to write down the above statement about you!)

Your purpose is the very gift that someone who lost their way is waiting for.

In order to be a gift you must grab new opportunities as they come.

When I say YOU and ONLY YOU have the opportunity to change your life its true.

Do you feel it now?

If I can get you to hone in on your positive feelings and transmit those same feelings into action……You are ready to fulfill and complete your purpose.

You might be feeling like you deserve better then what you are getting out of life right now……

It's good you feel like that…because I'm telling you….THAT YOU DO…deserve better.

No matter how good you got it or how bad you got it right now.

You should always desire more, give more, accomplish more, and help more.

Write down…….right here……………what your purpose is!

I would love to do: (what)

______________________________________________

______________________________________________

______________________________________________

I AM PERFECTLY AND WONDERFULLY MADE AND POWERFUL BEYOND MEASURE!

________________________________________________________

(Don't forget to write down the above statement about you!)

Now whatever you wrote on the line,

I want you to state that very statement every day but I want you to say it like this,

I ________________________ (your name) will accomplish _______________ (your purpose or goal)by date _______________ and once I accomplish this I will make ____________________ (specific dollar amount).

I will give ____________________________ (what your are going to give back) in return for allowing me to accomplish my purpose.

I thank you so much for allowing me to contribute to this world and I will give my talents back to the world to help others before I die.

Say and write this statement down where you can see it at all times.

You can make up your own statement but be specific.

Once you make your personal statement .........please send yourself an email or text of your statement every night before you go to bed.

Let your statement be the first text or email you read when you wake up in the morning.

You just wrote down and spoke your dream, your desire, your goal or your purpose into existence but you may be asking yourself

Danyelle why haven't I accomplished my purpose before now?

(Don't forget to write down the above statement about you!)

I alluded to it earlier but let's summarize this book so far:

YOUR WERE BORN WITH A PURPOSE

+

YOU HAD EVERTHINNG YOU NEEDED TO FULLFILL THAT PURPOSE AT BIRTH

So it should

=

# Completion of the purpose

**So why haven't you completed your purpose yet?**

Remember you are loved but.............I HAVE TO TELL THE TRUTH.........

One of the reasons people are not allowed to complete their purpose. (NOT YOU OF COURSE)

Other people love to blamed others for the status of their life or worse they have blamed themselves

Now you know....... I will never give power to anything negative...... but we have all done it (blame others) for the status of our own life

So many people (MILLIONS) BLAME others for their failures in life.

People really think their life, no matter where they are socially, economically, emotionally, or even physically somehow is a direct result of the actions of others.

People have numerous reasons why they are not where they should be in life.

The story always starts the same, "You just don't know what they did to me"

You heard all the excuses I'm sure

I'm where I am today because of my parents, my job, my race, my past……the list goes on and on.

But the one thing is for sure they never place their name on the list.

No one will ever take responsibility for their own life.

This concept (taking full ownership of your life) is rarely seen.

You might have better luck asking them if they believe in Big Foot then asking them to take ownership of their life.

I pray I'm not talking about you in this section?

**Who are you blaming for your current situation?**

Maybe I did not name what or who you are personally blaming for the status in your life but I need you to know this:

The key to unlocking your purpose is to realize that............ whoever or whatever you are blaming...... **are not** and **could not** ever be the real blame for your life.

**NEWS FLASH**........People could never be responsible for the status of your life...... they **don't have** that much power

All the years, months, days, you spent blaming others was a **complete** waste of **your time.**

If you are blaming other people and you **haven't** accomplished your purpose before now then.......that's the **real reason** why?

**In order to be granted the opportunity to complete your purpose you must learn to take full responsibility for whatever is happening in your life.**

We are family right?

So I'll let you in on a little secret.

Everything that has ever happened to you no matter how good or bad it was designed to shape you as a person.

Another key to unlocking your purpose is to realize two more things for me before we move out of this section.

Number 1: EVERTHING you will ever need to complete your purpose you already have inside of you.

I AM PERFECTLY AND WONDERFULLY MADE AND POWERFUL BEYOND MEASURE!

---

(Don't forget to write down the above statement about you!)

I'm not crazy.......... I know I made that very same point before but I believe in that statement so much I had to remind you again.

Just as much as I believe every day we have left is a gift.

I believe everything we need to fulfill our goals in life is trapped inside of us just dying to get out.

Go ahead and ask me....

Danyelle you are telling me......My purpose is **trapped** inside of me and only waiting (for me) to let it out.

**Hard to believe......You are the only one** that has the key to unlock your mind so you can complete your purpose before you die.
**Hard to believe......You are the only one** that can rise above your current circumstance and reach for your destiny.
**Hard to believe......You are the only one** that can stop you from completing your purpose
**Hard to believe......The problem has always been You and You alone**

Just believe me please.........**you must** unlock the door to your mind and release your purpose to the world.

Will you do something for me right here?

It's another one of the side notes......

**I REALLY NEED YOU TO GET THIS**

I AM PERFECTLY AND WONDERFULLY MADE AND POWERFUL BEYOND MEASURE!

---

(Don't forget to write down the above statement about you!)

I want you to think about a baby being born.

Shout out to my mother's but I need all my men readers to get this analogy to.

Visualize something growing inside of someone……developing, growing, and getting all its necessary parts **without ever** being seen by anyone until the appointed time.

Have you ever taken the time to watch a pregnant women's body changed right before your eyes?

Her body has changed so dramatically from when she was 6 weeks pregnant to when she is 9 months pregnant and is about to deliver.

I'm a witness… I gained 35 pounds when I delivered my first daughter Jonneshia, I remember being a perfect size and shape before I got pregnant.

I literally had no belly the whole pregnancy until I was about 6 months. Then BAM it seems like it was overnight but my belly tripled in size. (I couldn't even see my feet)

At the appointed time on December 3, 1988 my beautiful baby girl was born.

Three years later I gave birth to her sister Whitney, and 5 years later I gave birth to my only son Jonathan and the same thing happen with all three.

(Don't forget to write down the above statement about you!)

No one would have known I was pregnant if I did not have my beautiful kids to show for it because right after I had them my stomach and body went right back to the shape I had prior to me being pregnant.

I was looking for a place to talk about my gifts from God and he allowed me to put them in this section.

I told you that when I was writing this book it was never about me but about you .....

**Back to my story**

My children were finally here and everyone could now see what I only felt growing inside of me prior to their births.

When a baby is delivered everyone who sees the birth and I do mean everyone is astonished both male and females alike.

For this analogy I want you to pay close special attention to the fact that **no-one sees** the baby until the day.....the baby is born. (Sonograms do not count for this section)

The pregnant mother **had to wait** 9 months to deliver her baby..... Some mother's say their children are the most precious things in the world....... but she still had to wait.

This section is designed to speak to the people who had to wait for your purpose to be completed.

---

(Don't forget to write down the above statement about you!)

Just like a mother had to wait for her baby to be delivered sometimes **you have to wait for the right time for your purpose to be completed**

Your purpose is locked inside you, being developed by books like this, by personal development speakers, sermons, whatever is being fed to your mind, body and soul is feeding and developing your purpose.

Just like a baby develops out of human eye sight your purpose is being developed inside of you (out of sight).

Guess what? No one has to see or believe in your purpose right now.

If your reading my book and your purpose has not happened yet........**only** means your purpose is not ready to be born yet.

Just because your purpose has not been delivered (released)....... does not mean it's not going to come at its appointed time.

I love to read the bible and writing this section made me think about the women who had the issue of blood for 12 years.

I imagined when she got tired of her issue she went and did something about it.

Just in case you don't know the story.....Let me summarize

A woman with an issue she had for 12 years went out (for the sole reason) to touch the hem of Jesus garment and she was instantly healed because of her faith.

I AM PERFECTLY AND WONDERFULLY MADE AND POWERFUL BEYOND MEASURE!

______________________________________________

(Don't forget to write down the above statement about you!)

What stuck out the most to me about this story and what gave me the most comfort was:

1. She believed she was going to be healed just by a touch
2. She didn't tell anyone where she was going
3. She didn't tell anyone what she was planning to do
4. She didn't believe she could not be healed just because she had the same issue for 12 years
5. She didn't believe that she had to go her grave with her issue.

Writing this section to you brought me to tears because I can relate to that woman.

1. You see I was shown….. I was going to write books,
2. I told people I was going to write books (33 years went by with no book produced),
3. I worked for people who didn't encourage me to write books
4. I had people who said I would never write and should not write because of my writing style.

But **I believed** that I wasn't going to die **before I wrote and published the book you are holding right now**

I'm talking about me so you may be asking

Danyelle what can I get out of this story this analogy?

I hope you got to be overjoyed about your un-completed purpose because you have not died yet.

---

(Don't forget to write down the above statement about you!)

I hope you got to be overjoyed because your delayed purpose does not mean it's not coming.

Learn how to look at your purpose as being delayed not denied by **YOU and ONLY YOU**....... and not by anyone else's actions.

You have to realize (once and for all) at the appointed time it (your purpose) will be born.

**Now guess what your job is to do in the meantime?**

1. Take care of your purpose **(feed yourself good positive thoughts),**
2. Develop a plan **write down your purpose and keep it in a safe place**
3. Get a doctor or someone that can make sure you deliver correctly-**Get a mentor and ask for help**
4. Then **JUST DO IT**.
5. **LET YOUR PURPOSE BE BORN**....... unleash your purpose to the world!

Just for old time sake.......

1. Say what your purpose is
2. Write what your purpose is,
3. Say how much your purpose will bring to you
4. Say what you will give back for being allowed to fulfill your purpose
5. Say who you will help along the way.

I AM PERFECTLY AND WONDERFULLY MADE AND POWERFUL BEYOND MEASURE!

---

(Don't forget to write down the above statement about you!)

I HAVE A REQUIRMENT FOR YOU. Can you do something for me please?

**YOU HAVE TO CHANGED YOUR PRECEPTION AND WALK AS A SURVIVOR AND NOT A VICTIM FROM THIS POINT ON**

**I alluded to it earlier but I have been directed to clarify my position......**

**RIGHT HERE RIGHT NOW!**

You must change your perception about why your purpose has not come to pass yet.

Please read and understand the analogy of you being a gift to the world pregnant with your purpose (whether you're a man or a women), and when you deliver your purpose it will possibly help millions or even billions of people.

You also and more important than anything I wrote before...... **have to** be ok with your purpose still being inside of you right now.

You have to do a shift in your mind:

1. First stop blaming others
2. Change your negative perception about waiting to positive
3. Believe everything happens at the right time and you have just been focused on the wrong things.

I AM PERFECTLY AND WONDERFULLY MADE AND POWERFUL BEYOND MEASURE!

---

(Don't forget to write down the above statement about you!)

So many people block the birth of their purpose because they focus on negative things instead of positive things.

This is going to be the most profound statement of the entire book.

**NOTHING POSITIVE WILL EVER COME OUT OF SOMETHING NEGATIVE.**

What I mean is that when you focused and root **all your energy** on negative thoughts and things.......... It's impossible to produce something positive.

**NOTHING POSITIVE WILL EVER COME OUT OF SOMETHING NEGATIVE.**

Let me stop you right now.....

Your thinking.....Is what Danyelle is saying true?

I know you instantly started thinking about someone who came out negative environment and became a star, someone famous, or even a millionaire.

That thought simply proves my point and I submit that he or she focused on positive thoughts and positive actions even though their situation may have started out negative.

I will never....... and I do mean NEVER...... give any of my power or energy.....to anything negative for the rest of my life.

(Don't forget to write down the above statement about you!)

**Learning to turn off the negative chatter in my head was one of my greatest accomplishments.**

If you are reading this book and your purpose has not been fulfilled..... I'm going to challenge you to do the same thing.

I need you to live, speak, and think my new mottos....

1. **ALWAYS POSITIVE NOTHING NEGATIVE**
2. **ONLY POSITIVE THINGS HAPPEN TO ME**
3. **I AM WHO I SAY I AM**
4. **I CAN DO ANYTHING I WANT TO DO**
5. **I AM CHANGING FOR THE BETTER**

**Imagine with me!**

To be successful in completing your purpose I'm going to let you in on my secret weapon.

The moment I recognized how much power I was personally giving to my negative thoughts and how they were affecting me as a person.

I created a positive light switch and I'm willing to share it with you.

I want you to imagine I just installed and attached a positive light switch right behind your right ear.

This light switch is very powerful.

(Don't forget to write down the above statement about you!)

This light switch has the ability to pause the thoughts in your mind.......just long enough to change the thought to positive whenever you need to.

**THIS IS A POSITIVE LIGHT SWITCH only..... This switch will not pause for your negative thoughts..................never**

You are the only person who can see this switch and every time something negative creeps into your head you must quickly hit the switch to the off position.

Think of something positive or a happy image and turn the switch back to the on position.

If the negative thought comes back then I need you to repeat the process **EVERY TIME.**

You wouldn't have to use your positive switch quite as often if you would:

1. Stop watching negative news
2. Stop reading negative news articles
3. Stop listening to negative talk shows
4. Stop watching negative TV programs from this day forward.
5. You must watch what you let into your conscious and subconscious mind if you ever expect to complete your purpose.

If you truly want to complete your purpose.... you must change your focus to positive and remember you are protecting your purpose or goal (until it's birthed).

(Don't forget to write down the above statement about you!)

This section....well.........I know I may have lost my men readers....... so let me use analogy that all sexes can relate to.

**Take another walk with me!**

I want to use the analogy of driving

Imagine that your entire life you have been driving down the road that will eventually lead to you completing your purpose before you die.

Now depending where you are in your life today

It's quite possible that your car (you) are broke down on the side of the freeway.

It's OK......this section is design to get you back up and running.

I'm here for you.....

This book should lead you to the place where you want to go (your completed purpose) if you let it.

You can say (through the pages of this book) I'm like the tow truck driver who has responded to your 911 call for help.

We have all been in that place where our real car broke down somewhere and we had to ask for help from someone else.

That's the beauty in living.

(Don't forget to write down the above statement about you!)

If you are feeling broke down, tired, restless or even lost your desire to succeed in life

I hope my book is showing you to love yourself and revealing that you are not alone on your journey road to completing your purpose.

**Back to my thought**

I was raised in Foster homes so road side assistance was not something I knew about until much older.

Even once I learned About Triple A, I still didn't see the value in obtaining it until one day I broke down myself.

Breaking down was one thing but I had to wait for my friend for over 3 hours

That experience alone instantly raised the value of having Triple A.

I feel some of you (like my car)_may be broke down right now and have been for years not just hours.

WHY? Could it be?

1. You didn't see the value in forgiveness,
2. You didn't see the value in your dreams
3. You didn't see the value in your completed purpose
4. You didn't see the value in thinking positive before now

Hence......your fake feelings of being stuck today

(Don't forget to write down the above statement about you!)

Can I talk about what could happen while you wait for help in life?

The waits.........

The wait seasons I had to experience lead me to a world wind of mixed emotions.

While waiting for my friend..... My emotions were anger, anxiety, embarrassment, resentment.

Every emotion under the sun was running through my mind and the funny thing was I knew my friend was coming to help me.

What about you?

You may be in a waiting period in your life right now.

Are you experiencing those very same emotions right now?

Believe me when I tell you.........There is an anointing in waiting.

We all want things to happen overnight in an instant........and really those overnight, instant things or emotional impulses that we all have acted on were **never** good for us anyway.

For this section......... I want you to thank yourself for waiting right now.

**You still have time!**

(Don't forget to write down the above statement about you!)

Let's just say your negative emotions are valid because you didn't know your help was one the way.

BUT IT IS so STOP THE NEGATIVE FEELINGS TODAY.

I'M HERE..... AND YOU ARE GOING .....TO BE UP AND RUNNING IN NO TIME.

**ONE OF THOSE SIDE NOTES BACK TO MY ORGINAL POINT!**

Being honest even after that situation I could not always afford Triple A. So I had to call friends in my time of need still.... they came and may car (I) was up and running again.

**Side note**: If you don't have people who will come to your rescue in your time of need............... then you need to change your circle right away.

There is a motto or maybe better yet a style of living...... going around today encouraging people to believe they don't need anyone but themselves.

**I don't believe that for one second**.

I believe the world is set up for you to always need help and encouragement from time to time.

**Even better**....... you will be given the opportunity to be the help or the encouragement to someone else in their time of need.

So when I was writing this book.......

(Don't forget to write down the above statement about you!)

I made a vowed to **myself**, **the world, whoever** reads my books, and **whoever** comes to me in whatever fashion, to help them in any way I can

My vow:

**I will do everything in my power to get them back up and driving again (living again) from this day forward.**

Another lesson..........

Some of you have made a vow to do something different but you are not committed to the change process

I had to fire my boss for my vow and those words to come to pass.

**It was my time to give my gifts and my talents to the world.**

1. I promise you (my reader) I will never drive by you because you don't have road side assistance.
2. I promise you (my reader) I will give you every good part of me to get you back up to completing your purpose".

Remember we are connected **you are my family**

Keep reading so I can continue fulfilling my purpose.....Which is helping you to complete your purpose.

**Back to my original point.......... I warned you**

I'm using the driving analogy because I absolutely love road trips.

(Don't forget to write down the above statement about you!)

I live in California so I can drive to the snowy mountains in the morning and drive to the beach in the evening...... all in one day.

While driving in my car no matter how much traffic I got

I learned.....no I really MASTERED the ability to focus and appreciate **ALL** the scenery before me........ no matter what I saw along the way.

While driving .....I learned how to safely focus on everything ...... even the smallest detail.

Everything I saw while driving..............lead me to being extremely grateful for what I encountered on my driving journey.

**GET THIS.........**

1. You must learn to be thankful for the drive (LIFE)
2. Thankful for the ability to drive (HEALTH)
3. Thankful for the traffic jams (OBSTACLES)
4. Thankful for the fact that you can drive anywhere (OPPORTUNITIES)

**Hint....**

You simply must learn how to be grateful for all things you see and encounter from this day forward.

When I drive..... I love to look at traffic and all the cars around me.

(Don't forget to write down the above statement about you!)

Believe it or not your eyes should not be fixated on the car right in front of you.

The DMV instructs you to scan from right to left from time to time while you are driving.

Are you one of those people who drive only looking at the tail end lights of all the cars in right in front of you?

**STOP IT......There is so many things around you that you are missing**

I'm not a reckless driver but it's not uncommon for me to even look at the people driving right next to me.

1. I notice people rushing in and out of traffic (sometimes the very person who causes an accident) because they were late to work
2. I notice people not watching ahead of them, texting, putting on makeup, reading, or even singing loudly while driving.

All I can tell you is when you take the time to notice your surroundings you will be amazed by what you see.

Another thing I do while driving is..........

I focus on all the trash along the freeway edge.

You are saying in your mind "that's it....... Danyelle is off", she focuses on trash.....

(Don't forget to write down the above statement about you!)

**YES I DO**

A better way to say it is……. I noticed the lack of landscaping on the freeway edge really drew my attention while driving.

I'm not really focused on the trash so much as me noticing when the landscape changes as I drive on the same freeway.

**You see you sometimes have to look at the trash just long enough to appreciate when the beauty starts.**

You may be a person who has focused on trash in your life…..but today…… I want you to focus on the beauty of where you are in life today.

The moment you learn how to be grateful for the change in the landscape (your past), and believe in the beauty you see all around you……..
**YOUR LIFE WILL CHANGE FOR THE BETTER**.

I've been fortunate enough to be driving and notice the change in landscape.

I can look over and see trash for about 10 or 15 miles but then out of the blue while driving on the same freeway

I see a beautiful set of flowers along the freeway edge

I quickly look up at the freeway sign to make sure I didn't changed freeways.

I AM PERFECTLY AND WONDERFULLY MADE AND POWERFUL BEYOND MEASURE!

---

(Don't forget to write down the above statement about you!)

There is an anointing in staying on the right road

**You see the city or zip code changed but the freeway I was driving on did not.**

That's just how it is in life……

YOU have to know you are on the right road and be determined **not to stop** when life gets hard.

So many of us stayed focused on the situation…..

Instead of being focused on the beauty of life……the beauty of the next exit……..the beauty of the journey

**Keep it moving please!**

From time to time……

1. It gets hard just to keep driving (waking up),
2. It gets hard to deal with traffic (Sometimes you may have to move at a slower pace),
3. It gets hard not to focus on your current situation(listen to personal development),
4. It gets hard to look at the beauty of the journey
5. **but never get off the road to our own destiny (keep living and striving for your goal). No matter what**

**Guess what!**

You are the only one that knows what your destiny is………..

I AM PERFECTLY AND WONDERFULLY MADE AND POWERFUL BEYOND MEASURE!

(Don't forget to write down the above statement about you!)

You are the only one that knows what you need to get you back up and running.

Let your heart lead you and don't be afraid to tell others what you need to survive.

When your heart **does not** lead you then it will be easier for you to take the wrong exit in life or get on the wrong road altogether.

You **should not** and **cannot** be the person that is driving on a road just because other people wanted you on that road.

**That road is a dead end in your life.**

**YOU HAVE TO LEARN TO GO WITH YOUR HEART**... IT WILL LEAD YOU TO THE RIGHT ROAD AND TO YOUR COMPLETED PURPOSE.

The road that you should be traveling on has to be your own road and has to be chosen by you.

Your dream, Your Desire, Your purpose is only determined by what is inside of you.

This should bring you overwhelming joy

No one has to agree with your purpose or your destiny but you.

Now.......let me....... get back to showing you how to reach your purpose.

(Don't forget to write down the above statement about you!)

I submit that a reason (**not the sole reason**) you have not fulfilled your purpose yet is because you're traveling to your completed purpose and you're NOT staying focused on your goal.

1. Your mind may be fixated on the trash you encountered (your past).
2. Your mind may be fixated on the accidents you encountered (life happens).
3. Your mind may be fixated on the people screaming out the window to move out of their way (negative people),
4. Your mind may be fixated on the radio news telling you there is a traffic jam ahead (negative news).

Whatever you have allowed to occupy your mind you unconsciously have allowed that image to occupy your life.

Whatever occupies your mind has caused you to STOP your car (YOUR PURPOSE) altogether every time something goes wrong in your life.

**We are family so I have to be honest in love.**

When you stay fixated on negative images you will NEVER and **I DO MEAN NEVER ACOMPLISH YOUR GOALS.**

You see the beauty in life and driving is to **keep it moving**.

If you are using the map you were born with..... You will reach your purpose faster.

I AM PERFECTLY AND WONDERFULLY MADE AND POWERFUL BEYOND MEASURE!

---

(Don't forget to write down the above statement about you!)

The original map YOUR GIFTS & TALENTS are symbolic and necessary tools for you to reach your purpose before you die.

I have to state it again "**you were born with your positive map**", which means you and you alone have everything necessary to fulfill your purpose.

You may not have unlocked the door or vision that allows your purpose to be revealed to you.

But know your purpose was given to you at birth and you are the only one who processes the key.

Now....... your inner positive map or key can be altered by society and by what you believe about you.

If and when you follow the map given to you by the Creator and not the altered blueprint map you have created.............You will always get to your purpose.

**ALWAYS**

Now you may have been rushing through life and jumped in the car without focusing on your original map and got stuck in a traffic jam called life.

Its ok...... traffic jams are better then you will ever know.

You would learn to appreciate a traffic jam if you knew before you got on that very same freeway that there was going to a 100 car pileup right ahead of you.

(Don't forget to write down the above statement about you!)

You are not one of the cars in the accident because you are one of the cars stuck in the traffic jam getting on the freeway.

How blessed are you?

You missed the accident all together and were able to drive by.

How many times have you been allowed to drive by an accident getting to where you were going?

As soon as you pass the accident the first thing that popped into your mind was anger.

You're mad because people slowed down to see the accident. People may have slowed down to pray but non-the less you're mad

The first thing that should have popped into your head is gratitude that you were not in the accident.

You **never gave** thanks or realized the awesome gift that was given to you just by allowing you to drive pass by the accident and not be a part of the accident.

**Let's compare this analogy to your life.**

You may have come through some terrible accidents on your journey to completing your purpose however you still need to be thankful.

That same accident (YOUR PAST) killed other people BUT only slowed you down

(Don't forget to write down the above statement about you!)

Your past mistakes did not stop you.

Each of us has the opportunity to travel to completing our purpose by taking one or two roads.

Now most people think and we are taught that there are several ways to get to the same destination.

I happen to think that's **not true** for all things.

You will either have to keep striving through all obstacles or you will have to keep complaining.

One road works and one road does not

I happen to think we have to stay on course.

It's just like the story I told you about driving on the freeway (the city or zip codes will change) but the road (the freeway) remains the same.

If you get anything out of this section please get........

To just be grateful while you are driving (living) through life no matter what.

All your stops no matter why you are stopped are really just for routine maintenance.

Your stops will not to derail you off your course altogether from this point on.

**Follow me here!**

In order for you to use the positive map given to us at birth...... you will be required to do things in a certain why.

If you do things is a certain way you are granted the ability to pass through the traffic jams in life even though other calls are stopped.

You may be allowed help the other cars (PEOPLE) that broke down on the side of the road but you **can't ever** stop doing you because you are helping them.

Some of you have stop on someone else's road. All the drama this road is causing you is not even worth it.....

Helping other people is actually a requirement but living their drama is not.

**I'm going to need you to focus right here........**

As you are driving to your purpose think about this...

You **wouldn't** run over a person walking in front of your car RIGHT? Nor would you walk right in front of a car that is driving at a high speed right?

There are going to be times that you have to stop in life....

Let's just be real and look at when a stop in life is good or bad for us.

I AM PERFECTLY AND WONDERFULLY MADE AND POWERFUL BEYOND MEASURE!

---

(Don't forget to write down the above statement about you!)

Consider there will some things you are required to do on your journey:

1. Keep yourself clean and keep yourself free from negative talk.
2. If you must stop and gas up your car(mind)……put good food in your body, remind yourself who you are……. and play positive personal development videos
3. You must give to someone at every stop you take, even when you are going through something yourself (give your way out)
4. You must follow the people who have learned what to do in the traffic jams of life, (get a mentor)
5. You must be grateful for the car(your life, your beautiful body, your direction and your ability)
6. You must thank the people who caused a little finder bender along your journey (forgive others and you will be forgiven)

If you do the things stated above……. you will be placed back on the right road and granted the ability to complete your purpose before you die.

Now I cannot talk about the right road without talking about the wrong road.

Keep in mind though I will never give room too negatively so this section will be very short.

(Don't forget to write down the above statement about you!)

There is another road and sadly there are so many (millions) of people are on this road.

1. People all over the world have traded in their personal positive map (their goal and desires) and took someone else's negative map.
2. People all over the world have continually been filled up with bad gas (BAD THOUGHTS) at every stop in life.
3. People all over the world have learned to live and operate based on what others feel they should be doing.

Remember GOD said you can have in life whatever you believe you can have.

You can have the life of your dreams or you can have the life that belongs to someone else. The choice is yours.

This road (your road possibly) is filled with ordinary cars, ordinary daily routines

These are the cars (people) who rush to work, rush to grocery store, rush to watch the news, rush to sit around talking negatively about people every single day.

You know the people who talk negative about everything

1. They talk about the job
2. Talk about the police force
3. Talk about the Supervisor
4. Talk about the Government
5. Talk the President

(Don't forget to write down the above statement about you!)

They just talk talk........... talk talk talk .......then they rush to go to bed and start their ordinary drive (talk) all over again.

They will call you tomorrow with the same old talk.

They're just driving around with no direction and no purpose in life.

When you don't have any direction and you spend countless hours talking negative about things their road will eventually end (death) = unfulfilled purpose

This road......this (life)..... is a dead end!

There are millions of people on this same road, there is a traffic jam and an accident everyday all day (sadly some of the accidents are the ones they created in their own mind).

You see those people or you may even be one of them that get in the car at the same time **every day,** stop to get coffee or something to eat at the same time **every day**, get on the same freeway exit **every day**, and wait in the same traffic **every day**.

There are people that know **every day** there is going to be traffic and never try to take a different route.

They just have accepted the false reality that it takes them 2 hours to get home even when there may be a better way.

**News flash**!.......There are computer apps that tell you alternate routes and you could be home sooner if you would just utilize the tools you have access to today.

(Don't forget to write down the above statement about you!)

It's possible you have become immune to them because they are so common or you may be traveling down that same road yourself.

Imagine with me ........

As far as your eyes can see........You can see millions of cars (people) with headlights and break lights for miles and miles.

What if I told you even though you can see the lights........These cars are not moving........ They can't.

There are cars (people) where everything looks like it works because you see the lights on but nothing else really works.

You can see the lights or you can see the person and you automatically believe the car(person) is running OK but they are not running at all.

Really the lights work because the only thing is under the hood is a battery and the only thing attached is the head lights and break lights.

Deep huh?.....

Most of us are surrounded by cars (people) without anything but the battery attached to their lights (their mind).

They have given up their soul, their passion, their desire to fight and their desire to win in life.

These people have been told negative things all their life and tragically they believed what they were told.

(Don't forget to write down the above statement about you!)

They have stopped looking at the new scenery of life and only stay fixated on a scene they passed so many times before.

The sad part is some people have passed that same scenery (in their minds) so many times they really never realize the fact that their holding on to their past for over 15 -20 years.

**Hint:**

**It's time to let go but......**

They refused to let go......

Sadly...... all they really had to do....... was push their windshield wipers to clear off the dirt, grime, and bugs that hit their windshield (MIND) over the years and they would be able to see the real beauty of life.

Once you clear out your mind .......your eyes **will have** the ability to see the other side of the road......the other side life.........that can be so beautiful.

The reality is at some point........ The accidents and traffic jams in life do end...... but for some people by the time they realize that fact................. it's too late.

These are the cars (people) you encounter who do nothing but talk about their past every time you see them.

They are no longer in the accident but survivors of the accident but they don't realize it and **you don't remind them.**

(Don't forget to write down the above statement about you!)

These are the people you see on the talk shows or the people who every time you encounter them want to talk about that bad relationship, that bad boss, their bad kids, the list goes on and on.

The people who allow them to speak about their past (possibly you) are just as bad as them.

You should not allow people to keep repeating and reliving their past period.

**Something in you likes drama.**

I may be the only one who will ever say this statement to you.

**LISTEN TO DRAMA AND EVENTUALLY YOUR LIFE WILL HAVE DRAMA IN IT.**

I believe there is a transfer of spirits so you better be careful what you allow around you. Watch what and who you allow to entertain you.

If you don't believe me........... I want you to examine yourself after you have watched a negative reality TV show or allowed your longtime friend to tell you more about his or her problems.

If you are not careful....... you will have an attitude and be just as mad about a situation that is not yours.

Deep huh ......just watch yourself and you will see.

Learn how protect the anointing and you will be one step closer to completing your purpose.

(Don't forget to write down the above statement about you!)

What I mean is....Don't get upset over situations that don't belong to you. It's that simple

Did you notice I wrote about this section trying not to use you as much as possible?

**It is someone else on that road I pray**

**It's not you from this point on in your life.**

Remember you are **already** on the **right** road to completing your purpose so now start to monitor your distractions (their situations) from this point on.

YOU may have to travel on the same roads as them at times in life but what separates the people who get off dead-end roads and people who remain on dead-end roads is what they do while driving(living).

If you are on the road to completing your purpose and you take an alternate route just for a short time or you encounter an accident (a mistake you have made) along the way. Do the following as quickly as you can

1. You must stop(don't ignore the issue)
2. You must get your mind right (forgive yourself and move on)
3. You must get off at the nearest exit(remove yourself or stop the negative behavior)
4. You must try to help someone else(apologize to the people you included in your situation)
5. Than just move on and go right back to working on your purpose.

I AM PERFECTLY AND WONDERFULLY MADE AND POWERFUL BEYOND MEASURE!

(Don't forget to write down the above statement about you!)

If you are the person talking negative about your past and you decided today that you not going to participate anymore.......email me I want to hear from you because I'm going to ask you to do somethings for me.

If this is you:

First.......Call the person you been venting to and apologize
Second...Thank them for listening to you
Third......Inform them about your change (no more negative talk)
Fourth... Ask them to join you on your new "**positive never negative** "road.

Who did you have to call? ______________________________
Did they agree to get on the right road with you? Yes _____ No _____
Date: ______________________________________________

If yes.......... keep them in your circle

If NO....Then note every time they call (every single time) they call from this day forward I want you to take a mental snapshot.

If their conversation starts off negative then I want you to introduce them to the dial tone quickly.

Don't answer the phone when they try to call back.

Blame it on a bad signal or whatever but don't talk to them for at least 2 hours.

Try it....you will thank me later

(Don't forget to write down the above statement about you!)

After the 2 hours listen to the tone of their voice……they are not going to be as animated as they were when they first tried to call you.

Now you can safely remind them that you are on a different road now.

The road less traveled but you cannot revert back getting mad over their situation (that's a dead end road remember)

Now by doing this exercise…. I mean every time they call you need to say the following to them…..

Hi ____________ (their name) I told you my telephone line is dedicated for **positive thoughts never negative thoughts.** I waited to call you back to give you the opportunity to calm down and see the bright side to your situation.

I need too much from GOD to go back to being upset for the wrong reasons. I have learned to be thankful for another day to live.

Be honest if someone said that to you…..How would you feel?

The person that says those words would be granted the opportunity to complete their purpose because they are not participating in negative drama.

I'm not saying not to listen to your friends that would be cruel…… but what I am saying is instead of participating in the negative drama remind them of something anything positive about their situation you can think of.

(Don't forget to write down the above statement about you!)

By helping them to look at the brighter side of things and staying true to your new motto you instantly secure a place on the right road in life.

**I'M READY TO INTRODUCE YOU TO THE WORLD!**

Not sure if you have notice while reading but throughout my entire book...... everywhere....

I've been trying to get you to change your perception, your mind, your thoughts, and your actions to positive once and for all.

The old you wasn't working right?

So let's create the new you.

**YOU ARE NOT WHO PEOPLE SAY YOU ARE**

**YOU ARE GREAT.**

I wrote the above statement just for you......

I created two sections about your changing your perception to positive because your perception is soooooo powerful.

By putting analogies in my book that you can relate to, literally everything I wrote so far, every section, was my attempt to get you ready emotionally to receive the next sections of my book.

(Don't forget to write down the above statement about you!)

I made a promise to myself a long time ago that I would try to change the negative self-perception of everyone who would ever read one of my books and everyone I would met personally.

Have you ever thought about the reasons why you feel so unhappy with your life?

The answer is not a hard as you think;

It's simple but people for centuries have always made it complicated (even me).

I want to offer up a clue.

Now let me put a disclaimer right here.....

"I'm no expert" and I don't claim to be....these are just my feelings

The main reason why you and so many other people have that uneasy unhappy feeling as you go through life that there is something better for you is because **there is.**

It's ok to have uneasy unhappy thoughts and really you should thank GOD that you never stopped having those thoughts of a better life.

If you only knew how powerful your personal self-thoughts really are.

The ability to have good self-thoughts, self-visions, and articulate those thoughts into self-actions are vital keys to you being granted the ability to compete your purpose and change your life.

I AM PERFECTLY AND WONDERFULLY MADE AND POWERFUL BEYOND MEASURE!

---

(Don't forget to write down the above statement about you!)

I don't feel longing for a better life is a bad thing however a good thing,

I told you some people thoughts get stuck in their past and their fears cripple their ability to move forward in life.

In this section: I want to talk to people who suffer from depression.

Now I know Depression is a real disease however I told you that I would never give power to anything negative.

I suffered from depression for years and I want to share what my depression thoughts did for me.

Depression is a real disease. If you suffer from depression remember to get professional help. **Remember I am not a doctor; not giving advice in any way...... this is just my story......**

One day I noticed my thoughts were continually making me feel sad and my thoughts would not allow me to see myself in a positive light.

There would be days literally where I did not want to get out of bed.

Looking back on those days......I lied to everyone and only did the things I had to do....to get by....and not draw attention to myself.

My family and friends never noticed for months at a time how sad and depressed I really was.

I became a professional on explaining why I did not want to do anything or why I just needed alone time.

(Don't forget to write down the above statement about you!)

It didn't matter that my husband just made a baby on me......Bottom line I was lying to them and myself.

Sometimes when you are going through depression you look for reason to validate your feelings and I'm telling you that you don't need validation.

Let's try something new the same thing I tried. Let's change our perception about our feelings for once.

When I changed my mindset to look for the positive in everything I encountered in life.

I began to feel that depression was a good thing for me.

It was weird to me at first

**I know I lost most of you right here saying depression was a good thing.**

**Depression was a good thing for me** and if you are really reading this book.

You already have learned the skill to see good in all that you are experiencing (including the feelings you created).

I created my sad feelings I was having........My mind stayed fixated on my past hurts therefore I created my current depression feelings. It was that simple

**I'm not talking about you**......

I AM PERFECTLY AND WONDERFULLY MADE AND POWERFUL BEYOND MEASURE!

---

(Don't forget to write down the above statement about you!)

I'm talking about me and I take **full responsibility** for everything I create.

Feelings are just that...... feelings....... and all feelings are created by you.....

1. If you have feelings of Anger you had **to think** you were angry
2. If you have feelings of depression you had **to think** you were depressed
3. If you have feelings of happiness you had **to think** you were happy

The list goes on and on but get this point.............. all feelings..... start with a thought.... and you can change your thought at any time hence changing your feelings at any time.

Remember to use the **light switch** located behind your right ear from time to time.

The first step in changing your perception for the better......is to start accepting responsibility for your own thoughts No matter what happen to contribute to them

I thought up my feelings of depression and I allowed them into my existence

A thought un-attended will manifest into symptoms.

For me at times......I had an un-easy feeling that crippled me into not wanting to leave my room or my house.

I AM PERFECTLY AND WONDERFULLY MADE AND POWERFUL BEYOND MEASURE!

---

(Don't forget to write down the above statement about you!)

I would be in my bedroom and literally having a battle against good and bad feelings in my mind on a daily bases.

I was using my light switch it seems like every 10 minutes

When I learned to master seeing good in everything that happened to me…… it was a life changing.

Looking back I was spending a lot time out of the house anyway……..

With work, exercise, kid's games, and College……It may have been time for me to slow down and just exhale.

In the midst of my depression feelings…….I would look round my bedroom and discovered…………… I had too many material things that others could use.

Only my depression feeling lead me to giving away my clothes and shoes to people less fortunate than me.

Out of this battle I realized why I was personally experiencing those depression feelings.

Sometimes you just have to go through things in life to help other people. I feel everything I have ever experience was to help someone else.

What are you doing with your testimony?
Are you using your past to beat yourself up?
Are you using your past to help someone who needs help?

(Don't forget to write down the above statement about you!)

By owning my depression feeling days my life changed for the better

When I could not get out of bed I began telling myself...... I needed rest......... and it was ok to rest today.

I began to believe I was not resting because I was sad but I'm resting because I was receiving instruction.

You must believe that all your feelings will contribute something good for you.

There would be days where I told myself:

Danyelle it's time to get dress, time to go outside and time to work on my purpose
Danyelle it's time to live my life, time to act on the instructions I received
Danyelle it's time

We all have experienced days when we feel sad or depressed....... just replace those thoughts with ......**you deserve** to have a sad day....... but you're not going to have one.

You can have so many **more happy** days if you want them.

**It happen for me** no, doctor, no medication, just changed my perception and I pray that **it would happen for you**,

The power of self -perception is real and you can make your day whatever you want it to be.

(Don't forget to write down the above statement about you!)

I'm a firm believer that our experiences shape and mold us into who we really are

You heard the saying what does not kill you only makes you better.

It really does it.

I have to make this alarming statement to all who are reading my book(my family world-wide).

WE ARE STRONGER TOGATHER,
WE ARE SURVIVOURS TOGATHER,
WE ARE CAPABLE OF SUBSTAINING SO MUCH TOGATHER
WE ARE GIVERS TOGATHER
WE ARE BETTER LOVERS OF PEOPLE TOGATHER

Think about every little thing that has to you happen in your life.

No matter how bad you think that experience was and then I want you to read those statements again and you will resolve the following:

No matter what happen to you
No matter what you did to someone else
No matter how much or how little money you have in the bank
No matter where you live
No matter what you have or don't have

**YOU ARE STILL HERE AND YOU ARE GOING TO CHANGE FOR THE BETTER TODAY**

(Don't forget to write down the above statement about you!)

**REPEAT ON PURPOSE……..**

We all have negative feelings from time to time. Feelings that something…. Anything…. has to be better than how you're feeling about your life right now.

There comes a time when we all get tired.

Believe it or not that feeling of being sick and tired is a good thing.

**Yea I said it "it's a good thing".**

You see family it's only at that point (feeling tired) that you will decide to do something new.

Some people like to say "**I've hit rock bottom**" and I like to say when you at the bottom the only place you can go is to the top.

Not up but to the top. …….the opposite of bottom is the top….. Right!

**You see…..I DESIRE you to have top moment's every day of your life from this point on.**

1. Waking up is a top moment.
2. Deciding to do something new is a top moment,
3. Deciding to forgive is a top moment,
4. Deciding to help others is a top moment,
5. Deciding to work on your purpose every day is a top moment.

(Don't forget to write down the above statement about you!)

**So .....Please get this......**

**Learn to be grateful for all your feelings, even the feelings of being tired.**

Just know you are about to receive your second wind.

There are better feelings available to you..... Keep in mind.....

It was your tired feeling that sent you out to search out this book.

Now back to you completing your purpose....... I told you I get side tracked.

**Let's go to work together.**

This book was written for the sole reason............

To give you the opportunity to change your PERCEPTION about yourself before you read the final page.

WOW that's simple right?
I could have said it before now....But I didn't so keep reading

**REMEMBER NO CLEAR ORDER**

All you ever had to do was change your perception and your life would have changed in an instant.

Now I wrote this book for you but I need you to do something for me.

I AM PERFECTLY AND WONDERFULLY MADE AND POWERFUL BEYOND MEASURE!

---

(Don't forget to write down the above statement about you!)

It's just another little exercise that will tell me something about you (my reader).

READY

I want you to visualize a glass of water that has been filled to the half-way point (directly to the middle of the cup), and quickly ask yourself is the glass half empty or have full?

Please check the box below in **pen** not pencil.

**I don't want you to be able to change your answer** and if this is not your book then I still need you to check the answer in pen anyway.

Promise me to buy your friend anther book and give them the opportunity to answer the same question. It's important

**You ready go.**

Check the box:

1. Half- Full ____________________________________________
2. Half -Empty __________________________________________

I am so proud of you!

By checking the box above you have now joined millions of people that were asked that very same question.

Believe it or not some answered the question in the way you answered it and some did not.

I AM PERFECTLY AND WONDERFULLY MADE AND POWERFUL BEYOND MEASURE!

_______________________________________________

(Don't forget to write down the above statement about you!)

Now I want to thank you first for doing that exercise for me! THANK YOU sooooo much

Can you do one more thing for me please?

Consider the following about the question you just answered:

1. Everybody(regardless of race or age got the same opportunity to look at the same glass of water
2. Everybody got the same opportunity to answer same question
3. Everybody saw the water level (right to the middle mark)
4. Everybody got the opportunity to be asked the question
5. Some people considered the glass of water half empty
6. Some people considered the glass of water half full

You can breathe now

I know you were sitting here saying I cannot believe she put that question in her book.

The above question was not mine but I needed to know how you (my reader) would answer the question.

I put that question in my book but **I'm not going to judge you based on your answer.**

I'm not a doctor or anything medical for that fact…. so my opinion about how you answered the question does not matter.

(Don't forget to write down the above statement about you!)

I can tell you...... I'm possibly the only person in the world that will **not tell** you or offer up a suggestion to what kind of person you are based on your answer.

I will however ask you to do one more thing for me and that is to have an **open mind** when you read the next paragraphs.

I pointed out the fact that every person that answered that question had the same opportunity to answer the question.

Have you ever considered the fact we are all given the same opportunities in life?

But let's get back to the water.

I know you are dying to know what I'm going to say about what your answer means.

Well .........

I want you know .........

Your answer means......................... This about you.....

Are you really reading?

A couple of lines up that I told you I would not judge you based on your answer.

I know you are looking for a reason of why I put that question is my book.

I AM PERFECTLY AND WONDERFULLY MADE AND POWERFUL BEYOND MEASURE!

(Don't forget to write down the above statement about you!)

Sorry I can't hold it anymore.....

It was a trick question because I WILL NOT join the other people in this world that think that analogy means something about you as a person.

To me and only to me.....I don't think the way you answered that question means anything about you......

**But remember it's just my opinion NOT A FACT.**

People all over the world have missed the greatest secrete and debated over that very question for decades.

There are millions of experts, psychologist, that have determined (labeled) what kind of person you are...... all by your answer to that very same question.

By far I'm not an expert,

I just have a simple Associates degree but since it's my book I want to submit my two cents.

I believe they all missed the most valuable point of that question ......I have to admit..... I even missed the most important point for years.

I walked around for years saying I'm optimistic, I see the best in everything just because the way I answered the question.

**Is that weird or what?**

(Don't forget to write down the above statement about you!)

That's how quick if we are not careful that we will take on others people's perception of us and for what.

A written, a visual test, or a question,

Wow have we really been reduced to allowing our answer to determine who we are as a people.

Side note: Your belief and acceptance in what the test says about you is what gives the test itself power.

All you EVER really needed to focus on is the simple fact that people all over the world, millions upon millions, have looked at a glass or water for centuries and been asked the very same question.

I want to imagine my test......I think it's called a beta test.

I want **one person** to be asked that same question every 2 years for the rest of their life. But the person cannot remember their last answer and they cannot remember they were ever asked the question before.

They would answer the question like it was their first time being asked the question every time.

I (just little old me) feel **the same** person given the **same opportunity** and given the **same question** while he or she is experiencing life will give a **different answer** every time.

Even though they are looking at the same glass.....I feel they would answer question **differently** at each stage in their life. I know I did.

(Don't forget to write down the above statement about you!)

You see that's not generally what expert's do.

They will track large numbers and asked different people the question but the people (have something in common) may be same age or race etc.

**Imagine with me!**

I want you to imagine being asked that same question:
At 5 years old at 10 years old, then I came back and asked you the same question when you were a teenager,

Then came back and asked that same question when you think you're grown at the age of 18,

I asked you that same question after you had your first failed relationship or after you lost your job at the age of 25,

Then I asked you that same question when you found out your job lied to you and your 401k plan (was not a vehicle for you but for them).

I ask you the same question after you ran out of money to retired at the age of 60.

I bet that your answer would change every time.

You see it's the same you but your environment your experiences shaped your answer.

So the fact maybe that you were right no matter how you answered the question.

More importantly……. It really doesn't matter what side you are on or what position your answer means.

The MOST important point is that we all got the same opportunity to look at the same glass, and based on our perception or position determined our answer.

**So many of us miss the value in the opportunities in life**

Think about this fact…….

All walks of life from all backgrounds, all races, and all social and economic backgrounds, rich or poor got to answer that same question.

That question has become a very popular tool to determining who you are as a person.

Think about how many people are reading my book and think about the countless millions of people who undertook that same test question at work, in school, in college or on an aptitude test.

What really stuck out to me **was not** your answer.

What stuck out to me is was the fact we **were all united** by the same opportunity the moment we were asked the same question.

I AM PERFECTLY AND WONDERFULLY MADE AND POWERFUL BEYOND MEASURE!

(Don't forget to write down the above statement about you!)

Now I have to stop again……. because I feel there are certain things that we have to go through because we are connected.

There is nothing new under the sun so no matter what you have gone through there is someone out there that has gone through the same thing as you.

This is huge…….. **You are not alone**….. This is another vital key

You **must take full advantage** of all opportunities that come your way from this point on in your life.

Learn to gain comfort in knowing you are **not alone**, your experience no matter how good or bad joined you with a perfect stranger who will need your testimony one day before you die

If I can get you to change your perception to positive by the end of this book my life goal will be complete.

I believe my greatest gift to you (my book) confirms the reason why I was born, and the very reason I had to endure so much in my life.

You are my stranger (my reader) and I know my personal stories and analogies I placed in my book are going to help you complete your purpose**. I just know it**.

I believe with everything in me that your perception of yourself or even your surroundings must change to POSITIVE.

You see once you have accomplished the art of positive thinking ….. You will be granted the opportunity to fulfill your purpose in life.

(Don't forget to write down the above statement about you!)

You will finally be granted the opportunity to utilize the rest of your time on earth for the very reason you were born.

I'll give you a hint.... I'm going to repeat something......

**Time is the only thing you cannot get back.**

Don't let anyone or anything waste your time from this point on.

Today make up in your mind that "**I'm not going to waste another second**".

Now you read it but.... I want you declare it

**"I'M NOT GOING TO WATSE ANOTHER SECOND".**

Think about it..... Really ponder.... how much time you have wasted so far?

Not just today but over your ENTIRE life.

How much time have you wasted on a dead-end job or in a dead-end in relationship?

How much time have you wasted watching TV, or not speaking to a family member or a friend?

Your **greatest possession** in your life.......**is your time**

What a way to start a book yuh?

I AM PERFECTLY AND WONDERFULLY MADE AND POWERFUL BEYOND MEASURE!

___________________________________________

(Don't forget to write down the above statement about you!)

We have not even got to the 21 day part.

I had to start with the above paragraphs to really get you to look at yourself differently.

Don't worry the 21 day steps are coming but I do have discernment and you are still **<u>not quite</u>** ready yet.

This book was written on my firm belief that perception is EVERYTHING.

Perception in the noun form is the **<u>SINGLE and ONLY</u>** reason for failures and unfulfilled dreams in life.

Negative Perception has hindered billions of people from reaching their birth given goals.

Introducing you to your personal perception about yourself was what the above paragraphs in my book were about.

The rest of the book will be my attempt to change your perception of yourself so you can live the life you dream of.

When you change your perception about you and your past that's when life really begins.

**<u>Your perception is your most valuable asset outside of your time.</u>**

Do you really know what the word perception means?

Could Danyelle be right?

---

(Don't forget to write down the above statement about you!)

Is my negative perception one of the reasons or maybe be the single reason why I have not reached my personal goals yet?

I'm glad you asked. I told you I'm no expert, however the dictionary states:

**per·cep·tion** [per-**sep**-sh*uh* n] Show IPA

***noun***

**1.**

the act or faculty of perceiving, or apprehending by means of the senses or of the mind; cognition;understanding.

**2.**

Immediate or intuitive recognition or appreciation, as of moral, psychological, or aesthetic qualities;insight; intuition; discernment: *an artist of rare perception.*

**3.**

The result or product of perceiving, as distinguished from the act of perceiving; percept.

**4.**

*Psychology.* a single unified awareness derived from sensory processes while a stimulus is present.

**5.**

*Law.* the taking into possession of rents, crops, profits, etc.

Read that definition over and over.

Read the definition and know what perception means in every version and in every form.

Let be the first to tell you that when you change your perception everything and I do mean everything will change in an instant.

(Don't forget to write down the above statement about you!)

I did repeat yes...... but it's important...... smile.......

If you can change your negative perception to positive perception you will appreciate what you have gone through in life.

The world today argues about everything negative so it's in your nature to focus on the negative and choose a side.

What would happen if you joined me and only focused on the positive things that experience taught you,

**All the time every second of the day.....ONLY FOCUS ON POSITIVE**

I mean it...

I need you to look back over your life and right now change your perception to positive about every single thing that has happen to you before.

Think about whatever situation comes to mind and I what you to declare
It only made me stronger,
It only made me wiser,
It only made me love harder,
It only made me be more careful,
It only made me grateful to be living,
It only made me know without a shadow of a doubt "I am able to withstand anything".

IT made you......the experience made you who you are today.

(Don't forget to write down the above statement about you!)

Just in case you forgot remember you are **PERFECTLY AND WONDERFULLY MADE AND POWERFUL BEYOND MEASURE.**

Now back to your mind

If you would believe me and accept how powerful your mind is and how important your perception is to the fulfillment of your purpose you would be electrified in a good way.

There are so many books, movies, plays, that try to show you how powerful your mind is and what your mind is capable of.

I love the movie Metrix.

The first time I watched that movie I instantly recognized how important and how powerful my perception really was. But prior to the movie

I like you never really took the time to focus on my perception or really utilize the power of my mind.

Have you ever thought about how people can be in terrible accidents every bone in there body broken and you hear stories of how they fully recovered.

Then you hear about an accident where no bones are broken at all....you cannot even see visible injuries however the person has internal bleeding or bleeding on the brain and they are pronounced brain dead.

(Don't forget to write down the above statement about you!)

When this happens(brain dead) the doctors immediately ask the family do they want you to pull the plug.

If the brain waves have shut down and are not working then to medical experts out there say you are not living.

You see your brain (mind) is the command station for the operation of everything inside of you and everything around you.

Your brain (mind) tells you how you feel about something you saw that makes you feel happy or something you saw that makes you feel sad.

Your brain (mind) tells you when you should cry or when you should laugh.

Those are just a few things because we all know about the nervous system and all that but bear with me.... remember family I'm no expert.

I just want to offer that we have the power through perception to override what our brain (mind) says about a circumstance or situation if we do things in a certain way.

Little old me..... Feels that your perception alone is something you have to get a grip on.

It may be your perception on a singular thing or your perception on multiple things.

(Don't forget to write down the above statement about you!)

Somewhere on your life journey to completing your purpose you perceived an experience incorrectly.

One thing that happened to you could be what has prevented you from unlocking the power of your mind and ultimately completing your purpose.

I want you to think about a going fishing.

I want you to think about **all the things** required to catch a fish.

For this analogy

We are going out for the sole reason to catch a fish, this is not relaxation trip.

This is not a getaway.

This fishing trip requires that you catch a fish so you can have your next meal.

Everything is closed, all stores, all restaurants, and you have just been told that if you don't catch a fish you **will not** get to eat.

Now this is not the show Survivor.

I'm going to give you **everything** you need to catch the fish.

I'm going to give you a boat, a net, a fishing rod.....

I'm going to give you bait, a map, no better than a map.....,

(Don't forget to write down the above statement about you!)

I'm going to place your boat right in the middle of thousands of fish all types to.....

I just placed you and your boat in the middle of a manmade pond

Work with me here.

**This is my analogy right?**

I'm going to give you everything to season the fish to perfection,

I'm also going to give you a fire pit so you can cook the fish.

**You have been given everything that you will need to catch the fish.**

Family I just lost some of you, because in your mind instead of seeing the gifts I gave you.

You quickly thought about well.....

I don't like fish anyway, I don't like water, I cannot swim, or you may be reading and saying:

What will happen if I do not catch the fish? (the answer you would not eat)

The fish is this analogy is your (purpose)

You immediately thought something was missing instead of focusing on what I gave you.

(Don't forget to write down the above statement about you!)

**FOR THE RECORD**
**NOTHING WAS MISSING.....**

**YOU COULD HAVE USED THE NET AND THE FISH WOULD HAVE JUST JUMPED IN.**

But you did what thousands possible millions of people do when asked to complete a task.

Instead of doing the task at hand you analyzed everything before you even started fishing (started working on your purpose).

Whatever you think..... In all circumstances for every task.....will determine if you will complete the task....... or fail the task.

We are talking about your perception......

So if you are given everything above are you still wondering if you caught the fish?

For this section I'm going to say..........

**SORRY TO SAY......... NO**

You did not catch the fish....... (YOU DID NOT REACH YOUR PURPOSE)

OR

BETTER YET YOU CAUGHT THE FISH (YOUR PURPOSE)

I AM PERFECTLY AND WONDERFULLY MADE AND POWERFUL BEYOND MEASURE!

---

(Don't forget to write down the above statement about you!)

AND LET IT GO!

I used the fishing analogy because a fishing image is easy for people to relate to and fishing directly relates to completing your purpose.

Everybody knows about fishing.

You may not have ever gone fishing but I know you can relate to that image.

More importantly I have given you all the tools needed to catch the fish so why did I say NO........... you did not catch the fish.

I said no because you (my reader) may or may not have completed your purpose yet,

You may have thrown your purpose back
You may have refused to take a hand out
You may have refused to step on the boat

Everything you needed to catch a fish was given to you in this section.

I submit that everything you needed to complete your purpose was also given to you at birth.

So Danyelle if that's the truth what's my problem?

Thanks for asking ........The holdup is your negative perception.

I AM PERFECTLY AND WONDERFULLY MADE AND POWERFUL BEYOND MEASURE!

---

(Don't forget to write down the above statement about you!)

I need you to change your negative perception about yourself to positive only.

Why haven't you started on your purpose?

We live in a society that shows us how to do anything that we want to do at any time. We are truly the freest nation that has ever lived.

You have the internet, books, YouTube, radio, blogs; Goggle.... you have been blessed and saturated with the tools necessary to complete your purpose or anything you want for that matter and you are not utilizing the tools.

You see the only reason you have **not** completed your purpose is because you have **not** stayed focus on the gifts you do have.

Now that's enough analogies.

I have spent enough time writing on the importance of you changing your perception...... above all things you read....... this is a must.

The next sections are dedicated and written to place you in position to start and possible complete your purpose in 21 days.

If you really give the next sections a chance...... some of you will complete your purpose by default.

**Disclaimer: the things stated below are the tools I used to complete my purpose, which was writing this book.**

I AM PERFECTLY AND WONDERFULLY MADE AND POWERFUL BEYOND MEASURE!

(Don't forget to write down the above statement about you!)

My desire is for you to know that you will only get out of this section and this book what you yourself perceive that you will get out of it.

**I make no claims**.

Please.... I'm begging read the rest of this book with a fresh and new perception about the words you are about to read

Imagine the words
Believe the words
Feel the words
Speak the words
And DO the actions everyday one day at a time.

PS.

Thanks for reading my purpose I really appreciate you.

Now it's time...... for you to start working on completing your purpose.

The following sections were designed especially for you!

Remember you are my family and I need you to do what you for born to do.
Remember I wanted my book to only have 21 pages these next pages were what I was talking about.

These are the words I prayed and said about you (my reader) and will continue to say until you can say them and believe them for yourself.

(Don't forget to write down the above statement about you!)

I want to re-state no matter how rich or rich you are........ **Time is your greatest possession.**

Yea I said rich and rich for a reason because the same amount of time is given to us all. We all get 24 hours in a day so use your time wisely from this point on.

This section is designed to help you work on and complete your purpose.

It does not matter what is your current status is this section will help you because I believe:

If you are thinking negative about yourself.....I want you to start thinking positive

If you are poor rich now....................................I want you to see yourself as rich.

If you are rich right now....................................I want you to see yourself as a giver.

If you are a giver right now...............................I want you to see yourself as an educator.

If you are an educator right now......................I want you to share your education with the world.

Shorten the learning curb for as many people as possible before you die.

I AM PERFECTLY AND WONDERFULLY MADE AND POWERFUL BEYOND MEASURE!

---

(Don't forget to write down the above statement about you!)

Notice we never stop evolving and we never stop helping others.

When you change your perception then you will instantly become the richest man or women in the world.

## IT'S TIME....YOUR 21 DAY JOURNEY STARTS TODAY

To unlock your purpose there is a series of exercises in the rest of the book that helped me complete my purpose.

The next 21 days.......are designed to

1. Get you to see your purpose,
2. Get you to start writing steps towards complete your purpose
3. Get you to start living like your purpose his already been completed
4. Get you to start giving to someone else,
5. And lastly Get you to start helping others get to their purpose.

To unlock your purpose...... **you** first have to speak positive about you.....

YOU READY......................ALWAYS POSITIVE.....NEVER NEGATIVE.

I AM PERFECTLY AND WONDERFULLY MADE AND POWERFUL BEYOND MEASURE!

---

(Don't forget to write down the above statement about you!)

# DAY 1

## "I AM PEFECTLY AND WONDERFULLY MADE AND POWERFUL BEYOND MEASURE"

**"YOU WERE CREATED IN GODS IMAGE,**
**GOD MAKES NO MISTAKES**
**TO PUT YOURSELF DOWN FOR THE WAY YOU ARE**
**IS INSULT GOD'S HANDIWORK,**
**YOU ARE BEAUTIFUL"**
**UNKNOWN AUTHOR**

### DAY 1. "I AM PEFECTLY AND WONDERFULLY MADE AND POWERFUL BEYOND MEASURE"

Your self-image and your positive self-perception of yourself are so very important that those very same words have been strategically placed throughout my entire book.

This is a repeat of the highest kind. Repetition is the key to keeping you tuned in to your positive frequency.

So why did I put the same words here again?

Partly because I knew when you got to this point in my book .....You would be ready to make these sayings a part of your sub-conscious mind and a part of your life.

I AM PERFECTLY AND WONDERFULLY MADE AND POWERFUL BEYOND MEASURE!

____________________________________________

(Don't forget to write down the above statement about you!)

This is Day 1 of the 21 days I spoke about in the beginning of my book.

You made it

For the next sections........remember you promise me in the beginning of my book to only read **1 day at a time.**

What I mean is.

I want you to stay on **day 1** for 24 hours and then go to **day 2** etc.
The next sections (days) only works if you give the day the full 24 hours.
Every time something happens to you (that's not what you expected) you can only speak and feel the words given on that day.

You will be required to write down statements about you in the am (morning) preferably before you start your day right after your prayer, positive affirmation, or video.

You will be required to write that same statement about you in the pm (at night) before you go to bed.

No matter what type a day you experience promise me not to close your eyes for the day until you have wrote down and believed your night statement.

Remember to work on you daily....... **you** cannot leave out in the am or go to bed before you have your **truth feeling** about the saying that you are writing for the day.

I AM PERFECTLY AND WONDERFULLY MADE AND POWERFUL BEYOND MEASURE!

---

(Don't forget to write down the above statement about you!)

**Please don't read ahead it defeats the purpose.**

The saying I have included for the next 21 days were designed for you to master and control your thoughts throughout your days.

Your **positive expectation must** be paired with these steps to bring about the change required for you to unlock your purpose.

If you ever have a day in the next 21 days where you don't' believe the saying that you are on or you can't master your feelings then I want you to deal with the root problem instead of moving to the next day.

Go back to a section in my book that offered you the most comfort or just remember your light switch that is located behind your right ear.

Turn it off .......think of something positive....... then turn it back on.

Repeat the process if needed but every step for the next 21 days are necessary and they all work together for your good(your completed purpose).

Until you can master your thoughts and your switch to positive for 24 hours don't go onto the next day in this book.

Now my book is not make-believe.....

I AM PERFECTLY AND WONDERFULLY MADE AND POWERFUL BEYOND MEASURE!

---

(Don't forget to write down the above statement about you!)

I know you will have negative thoughts come up but what I'm telling you is replace all negative thoughts with positive thoughts as quickly as possible.

Remember you have the power to feel any way you want about any situation that happens to you.

For the next 21days try to see something positive in all the negative things that are coming and believe me they are coming.

Don't worry the sections from this point on are very short.

I want you to write or say the sayings....... until your feelings match up with the words.

REPEAT.......YES ITS VITIAL

At the bare minimum please say the day words at least twice a day in the morning and in the evening before your go to bed.

If I'm really being honest ......I want you to say them all day every day...... because it reminds you how powerful you are ........but I know that request may be too much .

I want you to write the statement down once again

**"I AM PEFECTLY AND WONDERFULLY MADE AND POWERFUL BEYOND MEASURE"**

---

---

---

I AM PERFECTLY AND WONDERFULLY MADE AND POWERFUL BEYOND MEASURE!

______________________________________________

(Don't forget to write down the above statement about you!)

In order to unlock you purpose, you must speak to inner self so that your perception about your self-image will change.

You already know why positive perception is so important .......if you were paying attention to the first part of my book.

But I love you so much that I'll tell you again.

To unlock your purpose you must perceive yourself as perfectly and wonderfully made and powerful beyond measure.

To unlock your purpose....your self -perception must be switch to POSITIVE once and for all.

I know a lot has happen to you but "IT" did not kill you..... so know that you are STILL perfectly and wonderfully made and powerful beyond measure.

I'm using positive words to speak to your self-doubt, your failures, your social or economic status, your physical appearance, and again I declare:

**"YOU ARE PEFECTLY AND WONDERFULLY MADE AND POWERFUL BEYOND MEASURE"**

Write it down again!

I AM PERFECTLY AND WONDERFULLY MADE AND POWERFUL BEYOND MEASURE!

______________________________________________

(Don't forget to write down the above statement about you!)

PM:

**"I AM PEFECTLY AND WONDERFULLY MADE AND POWERFUL BEYOND MEASURE"**

______________________________________________

______________________________________________

______________________________________________

**Remember family....... say this statement all day every day, say it when anything negative creeps into your mind and say it when anyone says anything different about you.**

I AM PERFECTLY AND WONDERFULLY MADE AND POWERFUL BEYOND MEASURE!

---

(Don't forget to write down the above statement about you!)

## DAY 2

## I AM NOT WHO PEOPLE SAY I AM "I AM GREAT"

**"LOVE YOURSELF ENOUGH**
**TO TAKE THE ACTIONS REQUIRED**
**FOR YOUR HAPPINESS**
**LOVE YOURSELF ENOUGH**
**TO CUT LOOSE FROM THE TIES OF**
**THE DRAMA-FILLED PAST,**
**LOVE YOURSELF ENOUGH**
**TO MOVE ON"**
**STEVE MARABOLI**

### DAY 2. YOU ARE NOT WHO PEOPLE SAY YOU ARE "GREAT"

This statement is also vital to you unlocking your purpose.

Again I need you to write it and say it.....but more important..... I need you to believe that you are great.

I want you to believe "YOU ARE GREAT" just like you believe in anything that is a truth for you.

**Ask yourself what do you believe in?**

Whatever the answer was gave you a good feeling about that truth right?

I AM PERFECTLY AND WONDERFULLY MADE AND POWERFUL BEYOND MEASURE!

(Don't forget to write down the above statement about you!)

Your same truth feeling I need you to have right here and about every saying you will read from this point on.

Don't make this part difficult the book is almost over.

1. If you are a mother and know that you love your child...... that's the feeling I'm talking about.
2. If you are a male and love your car...... that's the feeling I'm talking about,
3. If you are a pet lover and love your pet.....that's the feeling I'm talking about.
4. If you love you and you alone...... that's the feeling I'm talking about.

You need to think and feel "**you are great**" with that same truth feeling listed above each and every day no matter what.

Today is my day to complement you.

**YOU ARE TRULY PERFECTLY AND WONDERFULLY MADE AND POWEFUL BEYOND MEASURE......YOU ARE NOT WHO PEOPLE SAY YOU ARE....... YOU ARE GREAT!**

There are so many things you have endured in your life.

Your past proves you are strong and you are great.

Your greatness is really unmeasurable and incomprehensible.

There are very few things (as a matter of fact there in nothing) that you cannot do if you set your mind to it.

I AM PERFECTLY AND WONDERFULLY MADE AND POWERFUL BEYOND MEASURE!

______________________________________________

(Don't forget to write down the above statement about you!)

We have come this far together because I told you that you are not alone.

So now that you have changed your perception you can really believe that you are GREAT, operate like you are GREAT, and follow GREAT people.

You see great people do great things.

**TODAY AM**

**"I AM NOT WHO PEOPLE SAY I AM "I AM GREAT"**

______________________________________________

______________________________________________

______________________________________________

**TONIGHT PM**

**"I AM NOT WHO PEOPLE SAY I AM "I AM GREAT"**

______________________________________________

______________________________________________

______________________________________________

By speaking, writing, and more importantly believing this statement about you, you are feeding positive words into your self-image perception and granted the opportunity to complete your purpose.

**Remember your purpose is inside you just waiting to get out.**

I AM PERFECTLY AND WONDERFULLY MADE AND POWERFUL BEYOND MEASURE!

__________________________________________________________

(Don't forget to write down the above statement about you!)

It's vital that you believe you are GREAT, imagine yourself GREAT, walk and talk like your GREAT, and do things that only GREAT people do,

No matter what you have gone through or what you are in right now today.

**YOU ARE STILL GREAT.**

**Remember family....... say this statement all day every day, say it when anything negative creeps into your mind and say it when anyone says anything different about you.**

I AM PERFECTLY AND WONDERFULLY MADE AND POWERFUL BEYOND MEASURE!

______________________________________________

(Don't forget to write down the above statement about you!)

## DAY 3

## "I HAVE CHANGED MY PRECEPTION AND NOW WALK AS A SURVIVOR NOT A VICTIM"

**"FROM EVERY WOUND THERE IS A SCAR, AND EVERY SCAR TELLS A STORY A STORY THAT SAYS I HAVE SURVIVED"**
**MHAR**

DAY 3 "I HAVE CHANGED MY PRECEPTION AND NOW WALK AS A SURVIVOR NOT A VICTIM"

**TODAY: "I AM A SURVIVOR"**

______________________________________________

______________________________________________

______________________________________________

Stating vocally and writing the words "You Are a Survivor" really speaks to your past.

I will never focus on the negative parts of your past so keep in mind whatever you survived is not important.

What is important is my attempt to change your mental perception about the events that happened to you.

When you don't change your perception it's the same old thing.

Your mind goes right back to you being stuck on the side of the road.......stuck on a past image that happened years ago or even

(Don't forget to write down the above statement about you!)

yesterday......stuck on a past sore that you ripped the scab off again....

**Keep in mind this place (your past) is not where you are today.**

Remember the incident is not happening today and what's important is to keep driving or keep focusing on the positive thoughts about you.

Keep speaking positive thoughts to every negative thought or person that tries to remind you of that incident or that sore.

This step "**saying that you are a survivor**" is so important for you.

Having the mindset of a survivor..... I believe is one of our greatest gifts.

The survivor mentality is up there with how important air is to us.

We have all survived something and there is an anointing is being a survivor.

**The Survivor Movement** is real.

Being a survivor allows you perks.

You will have the benefit to help others
You will have the benefit to be connected with perfect strangers all over the world just because they survived the same thing you did.

______________________________________________

(Don't forget to write down the above statement about you!)

Think about all the Cancer survivors they are all connected because they survived Cancer. It's that simple.

**The Survivor Movement** is something that you will have to speak, write, and believe not only for the next 21 days however but for the **rest of your life.**

Negative thoughts of your past will always try to come up usually at the worst times.

Right when you are feeling good about yourself, or have somethings finally is going good in your life.......BAM..... A negative thought creeps in.

The key is not to let the negative thought rest, rule or abide in your mind or in your perception about who you really are today.

Remember you are a part of a movement that acknowledges your past but does not dwell in your past.

**AM**

**"TODAY I AM SURVIVOR"**

______________________________________________

______________________________________________

______________________________________________

For the believers.... the bible states that the enemy cannot do anything new.

(Don't forget to write down the above statement about you!)

He can only take you through the same things or issues that you have already gone through before.

**Well to all my readers........People do the same thing.**

How many times have you been reminded what you did or what you used to do?

From this day forward tell them

Yea, I did it...... but I'm not that person anymore.

I have joined **The Survivor Movement.**

When they ask what The Survivor Movement is?

Say it's a movement where all the members have learned something from their past mistakes

1. Learned to forgive,
2. learned to live for today
3. Learned to love themselves
4. More importantly learned to love others.

People if you let them will try to remind you of your past every time they see you

IT'S Ok....... I want you to quickly remind them that you are **SURVIVOR**

**EVERY CHANCE YOU GET.**

I AM PERFECTLY AND WONDERFULLY MADE AND POWERFUL BEYOND MEASURE!

_______________________________________________

(Don't forget to write down the above statement about you!)

Hint! Some of you may have just become a survivor of engaging in bad behavior.

You cannot get to your purpose doing bad things to yourself or to others.

Once you decided to change your behavior your character instantly changed.

Never let people remind you of who you used to be.

You cannot perceive yourself doing bad stuff either....... **only good stuff from this day forward.**

REMIND THEM OF **The Survivor Movement** ....AND ALWAYS REMEMBER TO REMIND YOURSELF.

PM

"I AM A SURVIVOR"

_______________________________________________

_______________________________________________

_______________________________________________

**Remember family....... say this statement all day every day, say it when anything negative creeps into your mind and say it when anyone says anything different about you.**

I AM PERFECTLY AND WONDERFULLY MADE AND POWERFUL BEYOND MEASURE!

_______________________________________________

(Don't forget to write down the above statement about you!)

# DAY 4

# TODAY YOU REALIZED ARE LOVED AND YOU ARE NEEDED

**"TODAY KNOW YOU ARE LOVED AND NEEDED THIS IS YOUR DAY MAKE THIS DAY WHATEVER YOU WANT THIS DAY TO BE"**
**DANYELLE DICKSON**

## DAY 4. TODAY YOU REALIZED ARE LOVED AND YOU ARE NEEDED

I want you to ponder my statement "**we are connected**" the only way you can un-lock your purpose is to know you are loved and needed.

Our connection is powerful and I need you to un-lock and complete your purpose so our world is better place.

Experts say to be loved is one of our primary wants and desires.

**Who doesn't want to feel loved?**

Look around there are millions of people out there searching for love...... when they already have love and just don't know it.

I feel the greatest example of LOVE ever displayed to each and every one us is that we are still living.

Today you received the real gift of breath

(Don't forget to write down the above statement about you!)

**You are still living**.

If you ever felt un-loved....... I want you to remember...... if you are breathing.... you are loved beyond words could ever express.

Our creator loved you so much that he gave you another day to live!

You must realize love one how much GOD loves you......, Jesus loves you......, the universe loves you........, the higher power loves you......, or whatever you believe in......loves you.

Every day you wake up is an example of love.

Whenever you are provided the opportunity to wake up or have the ability to lie down at night to sleep is an example of love.

**THAT'S LOVE TO THE HIGHEST FESTIVITY.**

How much do you have to be loved...... to be granted another day, another hour, and another second to get it right?

**WOW......THIS IS WHAT I'M TALKING ABOUT!**

This section means so much to me......because I was a person who didn't feel loved at times in my life.

I felt like no one could love me because of my actions or because what I was doing in life.

I felt **all alone** in a house **full of people........**if you can catch my drift.

(Don't forget to write down the above statement about you!)

Those thoughts lead me to my own DEAD END ROAD.

I don't want you to make the same mistake I did so know this.

You are love, needed, and you are worthy to be loved.

You should have accepted by now if you're reading that your past, your yesterday, your mistakes, nor your failures define you as a person.

There is nothing you could do in your past or today to make me not stop loving you.

I love you no-matter what.

If you don't believe me then accept the association with each day you wake up as an example of how much you are loved.

I want you to say this day is a new day.....
I cannot change yesterday.......
I love myself today........
I feel loved today because I woke up and got another day to get it right.......
I forgive today for whatever happened to me yesterday.........
I will show love to all that I encounter today........
I will be grateful for this new day.........

**<u>NOW SHOUT IT!</u>**

**AM**

I AM PERFECTLY AND WONDERFULLY MADE AND POWERFUL BEYOND MEASURE!

___

(Don't forget to write down the above statement about you!)

**"TODAY I KNOW I AM LOVED AND NEEDED"**

___

___

___

Think about all the things you have done in your life.... some things you have done.....MAN! You're going to take with you to the grave,

YOU AND I BOTH know.....

YOU WILL NEVER TELL **ALL** THINGS YOU HAVE DONE IN OUR LIFE,

So with the knowledge.........you and only you know about your past........you should have feelings of gratitude just for another day.

You are still here (living) and able to do anything you want to do today.

Feed your mental perception with love today if you have to.

If today (day 4) was your day that you were not feeling loved, then sit down in a quiet place and say the following:

Time to say....... I'm sorry
Time to say........I love me
Time to say........I'm worth it
Time to say........Thank you for my gift (time)

Remember time is the only thing you cannot get back.

(Don't forget to write down the above statement about you!)

We are connected so I want you to see yourself as an important piece of one big humongous jigsaw puzzle.

I love puzzles because no matter how beautiful they are, no matter how many pieces they have, you must have all the pieces to complete the puzzle.

No piece in a puzzle is more important than its counterpart.

Your life matters, your purpose is needed no one's life in more important than yours.

**Puzzles don't get completed if you don't have all the pieces**

Get this.

Each one of us is a piece of the World puzzle

The World puzzle is the greatest puzzle ever created. The World puzzle solved (every piece in its rightful place) is a beauty to see

This puzzle complete will have people pieces that once they complete their purpose in life their piece moves into its right place and is sealed

Imagine all the pieces to this puzzle. People who came before you and people who will come after you will all be a piece on this world puzzle the moment they complete their purpose.

Pieces that unlocked personal growth, pieces that unlocked poverty, pieces that unlocked world crisis,

Pieces that unlocked personal triumphs, pieces that unlocked books, pieces that unlocked homelessness, pieces that unlock understanding, pieces that unlock compassion, the pieces of this puzzle unlocked the keys to the greatest questions on our planet.

If you unlock your purpose your piece can never be removed from the puzzle. You were here, you left your mark, and you left your piece in its rightful place before you died.

Realize that you are only still here so the world puzzle can be completed.

Look at the pioneers who started the civil rights movement or look at the people who started equal education, equal treatment for all. Look at all our military men and women who gave their lives to protect our country.

Look at the people who are dead and gone........but their beautiful pieces........are still in their rightful place. They did their part; they left their mark;

I just imagine them longing for your piece to be placed right next to theirs.

Your puzzle space has been empty long enough

They are waiting for you to fulfill your purpose so your piece can be put in its rightful place before you die.

Keep in mind a puzzle piece can never be removed once it's a piece of the puzzle because the puzzle automatically becomes incomplete.

I AM PERFECTLY AND WONDERFULLY MADE AND POWERFUL BEYOND MEASURE!

___

(Don't forget to write down the above statement about you!)

I believe that we are here (still living) to leave our mark long after we are gone.

I believe with everything in me that we are all pieces of huge positive puzzle.

So today...... I need you to remember you are loved and needed

I need your piece just like I needed all the other pieces before you.

My only desire is that once you unlock your purpose, complete your purpose, and securely place your (purpose) piece in the greater puzzle that you then take the time to share with someone else so that their piece (purpose) can be added to the puzzle also.

**PM**

**"TODAY I KNOW I AM LOVED AND NEEDED"**

___

___

___

**Remember family....... say this statement all day every day, say it when anything negative creeps into your mind and say it when anyone says anything different about you.**

I AM PERFECTLY AND WONDERFULLY MADE AND POWERFUL BEYOND MEASURE!

---

(Don't forget to write down the above statement about you!)

## DAY 5

## YOU ARE WORKING TOWARDS YOUR DREAMS AND YOU WILL MAKE A DIFFERENCE

**"I MAY NOT BE THERE YET**
**BUT I'M CLOSER THAN I WAS YESTERDAY"**
**UNKNOWN AUTHOR**

### DAY 5. YOU ARE WORKING TOWARDS YOUR DREAMS AND I WILL MAKE A DIFFERENCE

Now you are ready to get another key to unlocking your purpose.

This key is a little different because this key requires you to do something every day.

You have received all the necessary tools required for you to begin to work on completing your purpose daily.

It does not matter whether you work, don't work, in school, not in school, retired, unemployed, business owner, athlete teacher, engineer, gas station attendant, movie star, author, store clerk, hostess, or in the military,

**IT DOESN'T MATTER WHAT YOU ARE DOING RIGHT NOW TODAY......**

**IF IT'S NOT YOUR PURPOSE then it's time to go to work.**

(Don't forget to write down the above statement about you!)

It's time for you to finally work on achieving your purpose every day for the rest of your life.

STOP……I did not say quit what you are doing………

I said work on your dream for the rest of your life until you complete your purpose.

There are teachings out there that say **you have to be sold out for your purpose**

I do believe that you do have to be sold out for your purpose…… but….. I don't believe that you have to create an unnecessary hardship.

To me quitting outright does not make sense.

You have not planned and your purpose may not come to pass quickly as you would like.

If you act based on emotions without thinking your purpose can be delayed and for many people their purpose sadly will never come to pass.

I got caught up in that SOLD OUT drama myself.

Now my mindset was a lot stronger than my obstacles but I realize not everyone is there yet.

Here is my story about me firing my boss……… Real talk

---

(Don't forget to write down the above statement about you!)

I was the Office Manager for a job making OK money just mining my own business until one day I was looking at a personal development video that told me I have to want my purpose more then I wanted to eat or breathe.

I was going through the usually work pains.

I had an owner who wanted the entire office dependent on her solely. That was not the type of office I wanted to manage.

That's the mark of good management is to want the office to be self-sufficient and run whether she or I was there or not.

The office was really getting on my last nerves daily really every minute of my day.

So I remember being in the shower getting ready to go to work

My husband was in the bathroom with me and I was telling him about what the staff was saying about my style of speaking in the unproductive meeting the day before

He did not know but I was really thinking about calling off altogether.

Like I said this office was getting on my last nerve.

My husband did not agree with me that's why I love him soooo much. You have to have people in your circle that will tell you the truth (that was free)

(Don't forget to write down the above statement about you!)

He said "well-baby you can be harsh at times"

You're a motivation speaker not an office groupie.

Still standing in the water "I got it" my revelation about my life's purpose hit me like a ton of bricks.....

Till this day........I don't know if it was the water.... The personal development video......all I can say is what my husband said was exactly what I needed to hear.....

I instantly had a feeling like GOD and he was telling me to quit my job.

Circumstances required me to be harsh at times on my job, but being harsh doesn't work in the workplace.

You know with harassment rules and all?

Harsh does work in the motivational arena, the arena I was born to be in.

When GOD showed me I was going to write so many years ago...... he also showed me that I would be speaking, motivating and helping millions of people reach their purpose in life.

At this point (in the shower) I saw myself speaking harshly to a large crowd, motivating and pushing them to their destiny

My motivational vocabulary was not working where I was currently working.....

(Don't forget to write down the above statement about you!)

I was trying to make a receptionist into an office manager because I knew I was not going to be there.

**Side note always train your replacement when you're working on your purpose because** you never know when you are going to have your vision

So long story short, I fired my boss on a Friday morning November 7, 2014 to be exact.

I took my resignation letter, my company cell phone, the office key, and placed it on the owner's desk.

I also sent out a text to the entire staff that read the following:

*"Hi team,*

*Happy Friday I just wanted everyone to be one the same page: I am resigning effective today. My resignation is on ___________'s desk.*

*I want to thank _________ and _________ (owners names)for the opportunity to create polices, train your employees and to contribute my talent to your business.*

*I feel I have left your business better then I found it.*

*To _________ and _________ (office workers names) thank you so much for your comments yesterday . I believe you guys are in the positions that you deserve to be in and this is your opportunity to grow.*

---

(Don't forget to write down the above statement about you!)

***Sometimes you just have to get out of the way.***

***I can no longer work for a company where I don't support the vison or the direction the company is going in.***

***I wish you all the best have a great day and a great rest of the year."***

I sent this in a text because……I was already doing the steps outlined in this book……..

I was already working on my purpose daily……

I **could not** waste another minute in a job that was not for me.

I wanted to write this book
I wanted to be a motivational speaker
More than I wanted to eat work or breathe.

Let's just say….. I'm soooooooo grateful that I had a husband Mr. Ivan Dickson that made sure I ate……smile

It's important to have a backup plan that's why I'm telling you……..
**Don't just quit.**

I have friends who didn't play it smart

They just quite their job because they were caught up in an emotional Network Marketing meeting and ended up homeless and borrowing money from me.

SO I'm saying again

Do not quit without planning.
Do not quit without leaving your job in a better place
Do not quit without telling the people you love who will be affected by your decision
Do not quite before you are ready

Now you may be working at a place you don't want to be.

Remember my analogy of the pregnancy...... your purpose is inside of you(out of sight) no one has to see your purpose until you're ready.

So with that in mind ......**I want you to do 5 things towards your purpose every day.**

That's right...... I said five things.

1. These five things have to be things that will help you achieve your purpose or dream.
2. These 5 things **cannot** be routine daily things or errands you have to do throughout your day.
3. These five things must be completed every day
4. These five things must DIRECTLY OR INDIRECTLY relate to completing your purpose.
5. You must promise if you don't complete all of the five things on your list that you will move the uncompleted item to the next day.

I AM PERFECTLY AND WONDERFULLY MADE AND POWERFUL BEYOND MEASURE!

______________________________________________________________

(Don't forget to write down the above statement about you!)

**AM**

**"TODAY I AM WORKING TOWARDS MY DREAMS AND I WILL MAKE A DIFFERENCE"**

______________________________________________________________

______________________________________________________________

______________________________________________________________

The 5 things you are going to start doing daily will ensure that you are one step closer to completing your purpose.

One more requirement to day 5(working on your purpose daily)

You must write the 5 things down each night **before you go to sleep.**

Yea, no matter what type of day you had.........you have to work on your purpose before you go to sleep.

This exercise will help shape your perseverance and ensure that you are giving more to your destiny then you gave to your job.

If a day goes by and you have not completed one of the 5 things on your list

It's not the end of the world......write the uncompleted thing down on the next day. **Repeat yes! It's important**

I'm going to give you some space in this book to write your 5 things every day down but you will need to buy a journal.

I AM PERFECTLY AND WONDERFULLY MADE AND POWERFUL BEYOND MEASURE!

________________________________________

(Don't forget to write down the above statement about you!)

**A PURPOSE JOURNAL,**

My **PURPOSE JOURNAL** will be released shortly but I wanted to release the book first.

By completing this exercise daily.......no matter what type of day you will **ever** have for the rest of your life...............you will always have something to pat yourself on the back for.

You are taking care of your purpose.....I'm so proud of you!

This exercise will give you strength and direction when no one else will.

Below is a sample of what your list should look like.

**SIDE NOTE: Never work for someone and be too tired to work on your dream.**

Real talk......... You should never be too tired to work on your purpose. Give yourself more than you give to others for once.

Below is a sample of my five things that I did while working towards this book and my purpose.

Good thing is.......I was already doing them before I quit my job.

*Date:* ________________________________________

1. *Personal Development* *yes__ No__ Comments:* ______
2. *Write in my book* *yes__ No__ Comments:* ______
3. *Go to library* *yes__ No__ Comments:* ______
4. *Motivate or give to someone* *yes__ No__ Comments:* ______
5. *Watch a motivational Speaker* *yes__ No__ Comments:* ______

I AM PERFECTLY AND WONDERFULLY MADE AND POWERFUL BEYOND MEASURE!

_______________________________________________

(Don't forget to write down the above statement about you!)

As the days went by.... all of the items on my list changed but one thing that I put on every one of my list.............is personal development.

I think you should start your day being grateful; watch something motivational, read, pray, do whatever it takes to get you into a realm of gratitude before you leave the house.

**If you were really reading then you should have no problems being grateful**

This book alone has shown you the importance of utilizing the time you have left.
This book alone has shown you the importance of loving yourself
This book alone has shown you that you are not who people say you are....YOU ARE GREAT
This book alone has shown you that you should start your day and end your nights with the motto **I am perfectly and wonderfully made and powerful beyond measure**.
This book alone has shown you to accept and speak positive personal truths about yourself day and night......
This book alone has shown you that you are loved and needed

Start completing 5 things everyday towards your purpose and believe what this book has shown .........**YOU WILL NEVER BE STOPPED**

BAM!......I told you your purpose would be completed by default **and it's just day 5**.

Now I have to be honest...... there will be times you may not be able to complete the 5 things on your list.....

______________________________________________

(Don't forget to write down the above statement about you!)

When that happens promised me if did not complete it you would write it down on the next day.

Know if you wrote it....... **IT MUST BE DONE.**

**Write down your first 5 things......YEA I'm excited for you**

*Date:* ______________________________________________

1. *Personal Development* *yes__ No__ Comments:* ______
2. ________________ *yes__ No__ Comments:* ______
3. ________________ *yes__ No__ Comments:* ______
4. ________________ *yes__ No__ Comments:* ______
5. ________________ *yes__ No__ Comments:* ______

**You see...... I snuck in personal development as your number one.**

**I think it's important but you can put your own.**

**PM**

**"TODAY I AM WORKING TOWARDS MY DREAMS AND I WILL MAKE A DIFFERENCE"**

______________________________________________

______________________________________________

______________________________________________

**Remember family....... say this statement all day every day, say it when anything negative creeps into your mind and say it when anyone says anything different about you.**

I AM PERFECTLY AND WONDERFULLY MADE AND POWERFUL BEYOND MEASURE!

______________________________________________

(Don't forget to write down the above statement about you!)

## DAY 7

## YOU HAVE DONE EVERYTHING YOU MUST DO TODAY

**"WORK JOYFULLY & PEACEFULLY, KNOWING THAT RIGHT THOUGHTS & RIGHT EFFORTS WILL INEVITABLY BRING ABOUT RIGHT RESULTS"**
**JAMES ALLEN**

DAY 7. YOU HAVE DONE EVERYTHING YOU MUST DO TODAY

**AM**

**"TODAY I HAVE DONE EVERYTHING I HAD TO DO".**

______________________________________________

______________________________________________

______________________________________________

An important key to continuing to unlock your purpose is to realize that each day brings exactly what should been brought.

It's the morning and you are already declaring

You will do all you could do on your job, with your children, with your mate, and with working on your purpose.

You will accomplish everything you need to accomplish today.. Nothing will be missing and nothing will be lacking.

**NOTHING ELSE IS WILL BE REQUIRED OF YOU TODAY**

(Don't forget to write down the above statement about you!)

There are millions of people that go to sleep feeling bad because they could not do all they wanted to do in a day.

I need you **not to be** like those people. Everything that you will **do or not do** today is exactly what should have been **done or not done**. Deep Huh?

Remember you are doing the actions required for today and you are still working towards completing your purpose at the end of the day.

You should always feel proud of yourself.

You have done all you could have done. That's it that's all.

**You cannot live in regret** and you cannot be that person who is busy busy busy but **never** completes anything and always feeling like you should have done more.

**There is such thing as burn out.**

One of your 5 items on your list to complete should be a day of rest.

A day with family, a day giving to others, a day sharing with others, or even a day dedicated to show someone love.

You have to become a giver in order to receive.

When you have done everything that you had to do in a day including your 5 items learn how to just be thankful for a day of completion.

---

(Don't forget to write down the above statement about you!)

As long as you wake up the next day….. You have another day to complete what you did not complete yesterday.

There is a beauty in knowing that you have done all you can do period.

You (my reader) just be grateful for your daily accomplishments.

Just like faith without works is dead.

A dream or purpose without an action plan is also dead.

The opposite is true

If you are completing action everyday towards your purpose when no one else is watching or noticing then your purpose is alive and kicking even if your purpose has not been release to the world yet.

Family you must see yourself (right now) as whatever your purpose is.

You have to walk, talk, visualize, and operate like your purpose is already here.

There is a personal power I need you to unlock before the end of this section

**The power of completion**

If you done all you can do than you completed your day

---

(Don't forget to write down the above statement about you!)

The day is over....learn how to **turn off** the world and **turn on** you.

1. Turn on........The complete and proud of what you accomplished today you.
2. Turn on........The wonderful and great you.
3. Turn on........The satisfied you,
4. Turn on........The working on your purpose you
5. Turn on........The perfectly and wonderfully made you

You can literally lie down at night and repeat those things I just made you read and your mind and body will relax. TRY IT

Turning off the world and turning on you is a requirement

You gave all you could have today so it's time for me to appreciate and recognize you.

**Imagine with me**

**What's your favorite talk show?**

**THIS IS THE ......... ____________________(PUT YOUR NAME) SHOW........**

**LIKE.....**

**THIS IS THE DANYELLE'S TRUTH TALK SHOW**

Put your name in the blank in capital letters (in pen)

I AM PERFECTLY AND WONDERFULLY MADE AND POWERFUL BEYOND MEASURE!

______________________________________________________________

(Don't forget to write down the above statement about you!)

This is talk show is dedicated to speak positive to you and about you for 15 to 30 minutes.

The interview has started and you have just been asked to rattle off all the positive things you can think of about you in 10-15 minutes.

Now the interviewer has just asked you to describe your completed purpose in 10-15 minutes.

Were you ready to give the answers?

I told you in the beginning of my book .......I'm not here to entertain you..

I'm here to push you to the next level in your life.

Your complete purpose will elevate your life status right?

So were you ready?

Did you answer the questions in the allotted time?

If you didn't

I want you to repeat this exercise until **you can** rattle off the top of your head positive things about you and your completed purpose.

Get up and the morning and do 5 minutes of positive self-talk...... in the middle of the day do another 5 minutes etc....

You get the point but do go to sleep at night with completing 30 minutes of positive self-talk about the wonderful you and your completed purpose.

**THIS IS AN IMPORANT STEP...... I PROMISE..... NEXT**

Start visualizing yourself already operating in your purpose.

1. What does it feel like,
2. What are the people saying about your completed purpose,
3. How much money have you made,
4. What have you given back
5. What are you smiling about,

Imagine yourself being interviewed by your favorite talk show or radio host.

You started out telling the host about **The Survivor Movement.**

**You started** telling them all about you, what you had to go through and how you are now helping others overcome their past.

Your interview is being viewed by millions people

Your story is helping someone that you don't even know.

Do you feel it?

Do you already feel like you have accomplished your goal and you are helping people all over the world.

I AM PERFECTLY AND WONDERFULLY MADE AND POWERFUL BEYOND MEASURE!

___

(Don't forget to write down the above statement about you!)

If you cannot accomplish your goal in your mind then you will never see the physical manifestation.

You are working towards your purpose (5 things daily)…. you are imagining your purpose…. well guess what your purpose will come to pass.

**So I say again…….. You have done enough today!**

**PM**

"TODAY I HAVE DONE EVERYTHING I HAD TO DO".

___

___

___

**Remember family……. say this statement all day every day, say it when anything negative creeps into your mind and say it when anyone says anything different about you.**

**"WHEN YOU'VE DONE EVERYTHING YOU CAN DO, THAT'S WHEN GOD WILL STEP IN AND DO, WHAT YOU CAN'T DO" CORINTHIANS 12:10**

I AM PERFECTLY AND WONDERFULLY MADE AND POWERFUL BEYOND MEASURE!

______________________________________________

(Don't forget to write down the above statement about you!)

# DAY 8

# YOU ARE A GIVER AND REALLY MADE SOMEONE FEEL SPECIAL TODAY

**"IT'S NOT HOW MUCH WE GIVE BUT HOW MUCH LOVE WE PUT INTO GIVING"**
**MOTHER TERESA**

## DAY 8. YOU ARE A GIVER AND REALLY MADE SOMEONE FEEL SPECIAL TODAY

On your road to your purpose another key is to make someone else feel special along your way

**AM**

**"TODAY I AM A GIVER AND I WILL MAKE SOMEONE FEEL SPECIAL TODAY".**

______________________________________________

______________________________________________

______________________________________________

This world is full of people, who are **not givers**,

People are walking around and believe they don't have enough to give. That's a meth.

We all have something to give to others.

I AM PERFECTLY AND WONDERFULLY MADE AND POWERFUL BEYOND MEASURE!

---

(Don't forget to write down the above statement about you!)

Have you ever tried to give special to someone? Yea I said give special

We should and can make someone feel special each and every day.

I made a vow that I would be a giver.

I made a vow to give to whoever asks me for something.

When I put that vow in practice.....People started out asking me for money.

God knew..... Oh Danyelle.......... She has no problem giving away clothes, food, but let me see if she has a problem giving away her money.

You see I made the vow and when you make a vow.....you will be tested.

This section is about giving but make a vow on anything.....you can make a vow not to get angry....or make a vow to have more peace.

If you make a vow on anything watch and see if you will not get tested in that area.

I would go to the store or gas station and someone would always ask me for money every time....... and every time I would always give the money to them.

**When I learned to give I always had it to give. (That is profound)**

---

(Don't forget to write down the above statement about you!)

**Stay with me!**

Don't be one of those people who drive by people and don't give because you think they are going to buy drugs or alcohol with your money.

Give without ever caring what they do with the money.

Be lead to give and you will always give at the right time to the right person.

My husband Ivan and I started asking for the names of people we gave to...

Ivan even asked what happened to them, they would tell us some stories man.....but we started asking their name because we wanted to pray for them.

It did not matter whether we gave fifty cents or fifty dollars we attached a prayer of increase over every seed we ever sowed in church or on the streets.

Some of you are only giving in the church.....Don't get me wrong giving to church is a good thing when it's a GOD thing

You may be asking Danyelle what's the difference?.

The bible's new commandment was to give and it will be given back to you.

(Don't forget to write down the above statement about you!)

I remember being taught "how will you rob God but though tithes and offering'.

I heard that scripture more than I'm willing to admit.....

I heard that sermon preached over 1000 times but not one of the pastors shared or disclosed who the passage was directed to.

They always told me about GOD speaking to David or Paul even when GOD spoke to Joseph but they never added that GOD was speaking to the priest and leaders of the church at that time.

I want to say right here and right now........... I believe in tithing so don't take this section any different than any of my other sections.

Sometimes people will try to find one thing they don't agree with and denounce the entire book.

Let me get ahead of the devil you are not going to like everything I wrote but know my heart was in a good place when I published this book.
For my non-believing readers "don't throw the baby out with the bath water" unknown author because you have come too far to turn back now.

This is just my story.

There would be times I tithed and times I didn't but when I gave from my heart was where I received my most joy.

---

(Don't forget to write down the above statement about you!)

I love my Bishop....Bishop Craig Ward Johnson who always said if you cannot be a cheerful giver then keep your money.

Believe it or not there are men of GOD who really preach the word of GOD....Men not concerned with getting your money but saving your life.

Shout out to my spiritual father and my church family because they really did save my life.

Now being truthful I went to his church for over 10 years and there was a time when I only gave $25.00 to my church and tithe to my family members who needed help and he never treated me any different.

You see my Bishop did not know what I was doing at the time but GOD knew what he was telling me to do with my money.

I was sending over 500.00 a month to my family and giving about 70.00 to the church and blessings never stopped because I was giving from my heart and following GOD's instruction.

I followed my heart in every decision I made in regards to giving and now I am truly blessed beyond measure.

Bishop Craig Ward Johnson and Cathedral of Praise International Ministries will be blessed beyond measure. You just make my words

They loved and prayed for me when I **could not** or **would not** pray for myself even when I wasn't tithing and for that reason I will forever bless them.

(Don't forget to write down the above statement about you!)

Please don't write me about this part...... this was just my journey...... I'm not saying I'm right or wrong and **please don't stop tithing or giving that was not my intention**

**I believe in the power of tithing and the power of giving**

**This was my** vow that I will give and tithe whenever I am lead to by my GOD.

Who is leading you to tithe or give?

Some of you are giving 10% but GOD is telling you to give 50% or even 75% at times.....Some of you are not giving to anybody at all.

Something to think about

All I'm saying is be lead when you give or tithe and who to give and tithe to

Believe me when I tell you......................I will never AND I DO MEAN NEVER argue about the word of God.

Just one of those side notes......keep reading

I remember before I made that vow to give I would go to the same gas station and same store but no one ever asked for anything.

Maybe it was the way I was dressed but I can honestly say..... I was never asked for money from strangers until I started working on this book, and made my giving vow.

(Don't forget to write down the above statement about you!)

Not only would people ask me for money but people like never before would ask me for advice.

I got the opportunity to offer positive encouragement instead of negative encouragement.

Yea I said **negative encouragement**.....

When your friend calls for advice.....what are you telling them?

Some of you may be feeding into the negative conversation instead of offering a positive conversation and the moment you do that you are smack in the middle of **negative encouragement.**

**SO STOP PLEASE IT....Side Note I was lead to write about you**

**Now back to giving!**

Giving is easier than you think and you don't have to always give money.

Being perfectly honest there will come a point when you will have to give money

So you have to **obtain money** to **give money** right?

Complete your purpose so you can have some money please.

Have you ever really thought about how much money you spent eating out last month?

(Don't forget to write down the above statement about you!)

Me and Ivan have to keep an excel sheet to track our expenses for our company.

Taking clients out to eat in 5 months totaled over five thousand dollars. Just eating out......How crazy is that.

I'm not saying you spent that much eating out but you can take those same dollars and feed the homeless man or women that you drive by or walk by every day.

I won't even talk about how many people you can help with your shopping money

It really does not matter what they do with the money some of you should be helping people period. It's not about you right here.

I give to them because of my vow but think about this........they don't know how powerful I am when they take my money

Take my money and you take my prayers attached to my money by default.

You see with every dime I give the following prayers are attached.

1. Because my money is in their hand it will multiply for them in Jesus name.
2. Because my money is in their hand it will bring about peace and protection in Jesus name
3. Because my money is in their hand it will bring about loving themselves first in Jesus name

________________________________________________________

(Don't forget to write down the above statement about you!)

4. Because my money is in their hand it will bring about forgiveness in Jesus name
5. Because my money is in their hand it will bring about new opportunities in Jesus name.

They don't have to believe in my god and they will never know what I prayed over my money.... But the fact is I'm powerful and so is my money......

**<u>Never let the outcome of your money determine whether you give or not,</u>**

I remember my husband giving to a 22 year old homeless girl who was living on the street.

He only gave her 5.00 dollars but he told her point black **"You will be doing better the next time I see you."**

Well we got to see her together......she was no-longer living on the street and was all cleaned up.

Remember we only gave her 5.00 dollars...... but when you attach an expectation of change and **<u>never doubt</u>** the change will come.

Whether you give money, a kind word, or food I dare you to give it with an expectation you predestined before you ran into that person.

You are powerful ......Sow your seed with an expectation that your gift will change the receiver's situation and it will.

I AM PERFECTLY AND WONDERFULLY MADE AND POWERFUL BEYOND MEASURE!

______________________________________________________________

(Don't forget to write down the above statement about you!)

We are connected so I need you to be **doing your part** in your communities,

I will do **my part** in my communities, and hopefully we will meet in the middle, and everyone everywhere will be given a seed attached with a positive expectation

We have a job to do.

It should be a requirement to give to the less fortunate. You will never get to your purpose being selfish and refusing to give.

**Start giving today**.

If you are not giving right now then add giving to your daily list give to someone within the next 5 days.

**PM**

**"TODAY I AM A GIVER AND I WILL MAKE SOMEONE FEEL SPECIAL TODAY".**

______________________________________________________________

______________________________________________________________

______________________________________________________________

**Remember family……. say this statement all day every day, say it when anything negative creeps into your mind and say it when anyone says anything different about you.**

(Don't forget to write down the above statement about you!)

# DAY 9

# YOU ARE THE LIGHT IN THE DARK SPACES

**'BEFORE YOU CAN SEE THE LIGHT,**
**YOU HAVE TO DEAL WITH DARKNESS"**
**DAN MILLMAN**

## DAY 9. YOU ARE THE LIGHT IN THE DARK SPACES

**Look at you actively daily working on your purpose……**

**I am so proud of you!**

I told you that your purpose would be unlocked by default if you are doing everything this book has taught you thus far.

Now that you are working on your purpose you are required to protect the anointing.

What I mean is…….you were granted the ability to work on your purpose so now maintain your positive position and really start to show others you have changed.

**AM**

**"TODAY I AM A LIGHT IN THE DARK SPACES".**

________________________________________________

________________________________________________

________________________________________________

I AM PERFECTLY AND WONDERFULLY MADE AND POWERFUL BEYOND MEASURE!

---

(Don't forget to write down the above statement about you!)

**Never hype**......... I don't want you to revert back to doing what you used to do.

**You must be careful doing these next steps!**

It's a known fact that we are emotional creatures and our emotions go up and down like an elevator.

IT'S OK.......but you must learn to control your emotions people are now watching you.

When you look around now you will start to notice there is a constant flow of negatively all around you.

That's why it is vital that you are the light in the dark spaces.

Simply put.......don't give in..... Better yet don't participate in the negative continue walking in your positive purpose.

You don't have to make a comment or even give any energy to negative Facebook, Twitter post, or newspaper headlines.

You are the light in the dark place remember.

If you participate in negative chatter (the dark) then you have just became a **shadow of darkness**......instead of the light you were created to be.

1. I need you to be hope to the weary person,
2. I need you to be the happy for the sad person

(Don't forget to write down the above statement about you!)

3. I need you to be the forgiver for the person who needs to be forgiven
4. I need you to be the love to a person who needs love
5. I need you to be the smile to someone who needs a smile

I really want you to imagine that you are the light in every dark place that is close to you.

Try to be the positive to every negative with everything you encounter from this day forward.

It doesn't matter what's happening around you,

1. You can be the person that is grateful that it's not happening to you,
2. If you are the person that it has happened to...... be the person grateful that it did not kill you.

Your journey to completing your purpose will always lead you to the opportunity to be the light in a dark place.

It's kinda like your purpose is seeing if you ......will always take advantage of the gift of completion.

If you focus on negatively then you **do not** deserve fulfillment of your purpose.

Remember you are a gift to the world and you need to always see the good qualities in yourself and everyone around you.

I AM PERFECTLY AND WONDERFULLY MADE AND POWERFUL BEYOND MEASURE!

______________________________________________

(Don't forget to write down the above statement about you!)

**PM**

**"TODAY I AM A LIGHT IN THE DARK SPACES".**

______________________________________________

______________________________________________

______________________________________________

**Remember family....... say this statement all day every day, say it when anything negative creeps into your mind and say it when anyone says anything different about you.**

I AM PERFECTLY AND WONDERFULLY MADE AND POWERFUL BEYOND MEASURE!

______________________________________________

(Don't forget to write down the above statement about you!)

# DAY 10

# YOU ARE NOT MOVED TODAY ONLY RE-ENERGIZED

**"YOU CAN NOT STOP NOW,**
**I'M SENDING YOU JOY**
**AND POSITIVE ENERGY TODAY"**
**DANYELLE DICKSON**

## DAY10. YOU ARE NOT MOVED TODAY ONLY RE-ENERGIZED

I'm no fool!

The greatest struggle is to finish what you have started.

You made it to Day 10....Today is a day to make sure that you are truly not moved by what has happen to you in the past only re-energized.

**AM**

**"TODAY I AM NOT MOVED ONLY RE-ENERGIZED".**

______________________________________________

______________________________________________

______________________________________________

What would happen if we took all the negative energy that happen to us in the past and turn it into positive energy that help heal our world.

(Don't forget to write down the above statement about you!)

I know by now (day 10) you may have encountered something that has hit you right in the stomach. Life may have even knocked the breath out of you.

That's what life will do at times and IT'S STILL OK

I don't care what IT is or what just happen today……you are better than what you encountered.

TODAY YOU ARE NOT MOVED by what happened to you ONLY RE-ENERGIZED.

The only way to remain re-energized is to keep your energy off people and on completing your purpose.

It's like you are wearing a weight belt……A weight belt that keeps you in the middle of your purpose completing pond

Remember I told you …………………I would never leave you on the side of the road.

So today is the day that I touch and agree with you. Whatever happened today still only made you stronger.

I don't care what you are going through mentally, emotionally or physically, you are reading this book and right now your change has come.

You should be already imaging yourself completing your purpose, You should be already imagining all the people who are grateful you completed your purpose

(Don't forget to write down the above statement about you!)

You should be already using your positive switch and are constantly casting down all your negative thoughts.

## You are reenergized.

You should be already completing five items a day towards your purpose
So now what's the problem?

Maybe it's time to change your circle of influence.

Sometimes it's important to watch the people who are with you on your purpose completing journey.

Everybody cannot go with you to the next level. One of the hardest things you will have to do on your journey is letting people go.

If there are people in your life that are not respecting the positive change you made then I need you to love them from a distance.

I have always told my children... "You cannot change people" however you can change how people deal and treat you.

I got a glimpse of the power a Judge has when I had to go to court for my son.

The Judge controlled the behavior and the entire courtroom no matter how big and bad someone was and no matter what crime they had committed,

(Don't forget to write down the above statement about you!)

Even people who did not have a case just the people who were there for moral support was also controlled by the Judge

He controlled what we could ware to court, controlled what we could say, He even had the nerve to tell us to turn off cell phones off (not on vibrate but completely off),

Told us to spit out our gum Wow.... He controlled everything

I thought to myself I have that same control.

You also have that same power.

You can control how people talk to you,
You can control how people treat you
You can control how people support you.

If they don't treat you right, talk to you right, support you right, and then just don't give your energy to them at all.

You can never make people believe in your purpose but you can require them to respect you as a person and keep their comments to themselves.

**You are re-energized........**You are who you say you are!

I AM PERFECTLY AND WONDERFULLY MADE AND POWERFUL BEYOND MEASURE!

___

(Don't forget to write down the above statement about you!)

**PM**

**"TODAY I AM NOT MOVED ONLY RE-ENERGIZED".**

___

___

___

**Remember family……. say this statement all day every day, say it when anything negative creeps into your mind and say it when anyone says anything different about you.**

I AM PERFECTLY AND WONDERFULLY MADE AND POWERFUL BEYOND MEASURE!

______________________________________________

(Don't forget to write down the above statement about you!)

# DAY 11

## YOU MAXIMIZED YOUR TIME AND ACCOMPLISHED EVERYTHING YOU NEEDED TO ACCOMPLISH TODAY

**"TODAY KNOW YOU ARE LOVED AND NEEDED NO MATTER WHAT. THIS IS YOUR DAY MAKE THIS DAY WHATEVER YOU WANT THIS DAY TO BE"**
**DANYELLE DICKSON**

## DAY 11. YOU MAXIMIZED YOUR TIME AND ACCOMPLISHED EVERYTHING YOU NEEDED TO ACCOMPLISH TODAY

**Day 11 is going to sound a lot like day 7 I did that on purpose!**

If you have been doing all the steps outlined in this book you are closer to your purpose then you have ever been before.......

Actually you already completed your purpose in your mind so I want you to recognize what could happen when you are walking into your purpose.

**Write this.... Then keep reading!**

**AM**

**"I HAVE MAXIMIZED MY TIME AND ACCOMPLISHED EVERYTHING I NEEDED TO ACCOMPLISH TODAY**

______________________________________________

______________________________________________

______________________________________________

(Don't forget to write down the above statement about you!)

For some strange reason everything may be going haywire all around you right now, and if it's not be grateful this section is in this book because when you have your day please come back and read this part.

Day 11 is when..... **If you are not careful**....... you will start to focus on all the crazy things happening instead of focusing on completing your purpose.

This is the day usually you have stop completing your 5 daily items; you stop writing in your journal. You stop using your positive switch when something creeps into your mind.

This is the day you may even hear your name over the loud speaker.

It may be work, kids, mate/spouse, friends, co-workers; everybody is suddenly acting funny....

It may be your mother or father it does not matter who or what it is...... even the pet may be acting crazy at this point.

It's only happening because you are past the half way point and really are walking in your purpose.

Whenever you are on the right track you will go through something's that will require you to look at the lessons you have learned in life.

Remember the devil can use nothing new, or a better way to say it is people cannot use anything new.

I AM PERFECTLY AND WONDERFULLY MADE AND POWERFUL BEYOND MEASURE!

---

(Don't forget to write down the above statement about you!)

If you look around at the crazy things happening really it's the same issue just maybe it's a different person.

1. If you had anger issues then whatever is happening is meant to make you angry
2. If you had depression issues then whatever is happening is meant to make you depressed.
3. If you had love issues then whatever is happening is mean t to make you feel un-loved
4. If you had money issues then whatever is happening is meant to make you feel broke.
5. If you had family issues than whatever is happening is meant for you to feel alone.

This is day is where your sub-conscious mind needs to kick in and you need to remember and use all the positive things you read and wrote down before today.

You never knew why I was repeating things throughout my book or making you write down certain things throughout the book until now

I knew by now you would have **something nagging** you or someone is on your **last nerve string.**

The feeling that you **are not** doing something right or that you should be doing something more will try to creep into your mind today.

The feeling will almost be like a buzzing fly..... buzzing around your ear when you are trying to go to sleep that won't go away.

That's the type of un-easy feeling you will have and once again it's OK

**YOU HAVE THE BEST FLY SWATTER EVER CREATED= YOUR JOURNAL AND THIS BOOK.** This is the day when your journal comes in handy......

TODAY go back to the beginning, middle or your favorite part of this book. Go back to reading your journal and all the things you have done up until this point. Go back to remembering you are not who people say you are. YOU ARE GREAT.

This is the day you will need to look at all the things you have done up to this point and be internally grateful for your journey

This is the day that you will know without a shadow of doubt that you are on the right road and that you have done everything you could do today and every day for that matter.

This is the day that just looking at all you have accomplished you will remember you another day is another opportunity to get it right.

**You will keep going....... You have done too much to turn back now.**

I AM PERFECTLY AND WONDERFULLY MADE AND POWERFUL BEYOND MEASURE!

(Don't forget to write down the above statement about you!)

**PM**

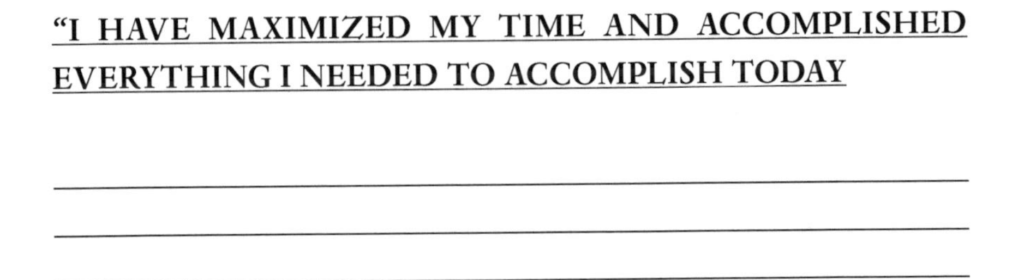

"I HAVE MAXIMIZED MY TIME AND ACCOMPLISHED EVERYTHING I NEEDED TO ACCOMPLISH TODAY

**Remember family……. say this statement all day every day, say it when anything negative creeps into your mind and say it when anyone says anything different about you.**

I AM PERFECTLY AND WONDERFULLY MADE AND POWERFUL BEYOND MEASURE!

---

(Don't forget to write down the above statement about you!)

# DAY 12

# YOU ARE SO GRATEFUL FOR LIVING TODAY

**TAKE THE TIME EVERY DAY TO BE GRATEFUL, THANKFUL FOR EVERYTHING THAT YOU HAVE, YOU CAN ALWAYS HAVE MORE BUT YOU CAN ALSO HAVE LESS" UNKNOWN AUTHOR**

## DAY 12. YOU ARE SO GRATEFUL FOR LIVING TODAY

Family I could have wrote a whole book on how important being GRATEFUL is to being granted the opportunity to complete your purpose before you die.

There have been a lot of keys outlined thus far that are designed to help you unlock your purpose but being **GRATEFUL IS NUMBER 1.**

The section I wrote about earlier in my book was only a snap shot of how important this section is to you.

**Come on walk and imagine with me for a minute.**

Imagine an entire row of labeled colored doors. . Believe or not this is a dream I personally had while working on completing my purpose.

(Don't forget to write down the above statement about you!)

All the doors are red and had huge white letters
I SAW:
A DOOR LABELED GRATEFUL
A DOOR LABELED LOVE
A DOOR LABELED FORGIVER
A DOOR LABELED GIVER
A DOOR LABELED CONTRIBUTOR
A DOOR LABELED STILL GRATEFUL

All the doors listed above you personally unlocked while reading this book

**NO...... STOP READING...... CLOSE YOUR EYES AND IMAGINE A ROW OF DOORS.**

There are five steps that you have to walk in a straight line to each door.

Once you open one door...you see another door..... And so on.

Now this book has been pushing you to use the keys that you were born with..... The very keys to unlock the doors that were holding you back from completing your purpose before now.

You have already unlocked:

1. The door to accepting your past
2. The door to loving yourself
3. The door to forgiving yourself
4. The door to forgiving others
5. The door to only positive thoughts

_______________________________________________

(Don't forget to write down the above statement about you!)

You have unlocked so many doors thus far and I 'm so proud of you.....but I would bet my final dollar that the **first** door and the **last door** and every door in between would be a door labeled GRATEFULLNESS in small letters right under the door title.

**AM**

**"TODAY I AM SO GRATEFUL IM STILL LIVING".**

_______________________________________________

_______________________________________________

_______________________________________________

IF YOU **CAN NOT** LEARN TO BE GRATEFUL IN ALL CIRCUMSTANCES THEN I FEEL YOU WILL **NEVER** TRULY GET TO COMPLETE YOUR PURPOSE.

(Remember I'm no expert) I'm just saying......

Life will defiantly throw you some curve balls and it will seem like it's very difficult to be grateful for everything that is happening to you.............

I cannot stress enough if you **cannot** learn to be grateful for all things that happen to you then your purpose will be delayed.

Even though this is day 12 for you.......... for me being grateful was my day 1

My refusal to be grateful for everything in my life was the single reason why my book took 33 years to come to pass.

---

(Don't forget to write down the above statement about you!)

No matter what new things you have encountered on purpose completing journey you must be grateful for them all.

Gratefulness is just a requirement don't question it...... just do it.

Please do a mental exercise for me right now before you keep reading.

Sit in a quiet place...... go to YouTube...... and type in water or ocean sounds.

I like the crashing ocean sounds but pick anyone you like.

1. As you hear the water sounds visualize you being washed over with gratefulness.
2. As you hear the water sounds think about having all you need right now.
3. As you hear the water sounds think about being healthy and happy

As I heard the water sounds I thought about my great husband my children my friends, I thought about all the food I had in the refrigerator.

It may be a small thing to you but I grew up in a foster home so me having my own home and food brings brought me to gratitude and brought me to tears most of the time.

I think about all the people who has less than me and I think about fulfilling my purpose so I can help them.

I AM PERFECTLY AND WONDERFULLY MADE AND POWERFUL BEYOND MEASURE!

---

(Don't forget to write down the above statement about you!)

Every time I do this exercise I have tears rolling down my face because of all the things I have to be grateful for.

You should try it.

Have you ever really stopped to ponder how many things you have to be grateful for?

Now I want you to take the time to acknowledge them and please include I am grateful for my completed purpose.

**PM**

**"TODAY I AM SO GRATEFUL IM STILL LIVING".**

---

---

---

**Remember family……. say this statement all day every day, say it when anything negative creeps into your mind and say it when anyone says anything different about you.**

I AM PERFECTLY AND WONDERFULLY MADE AND POWERFUL BEYOND MEASURE!

---

(Don't forget to write down the above statement about you!)

# DAY 13

# YOU ARE SO HAPPY THAT YOU ARE SPEAKING LIFE AND GIVING NO ROOM TO NEGATIVITY

**"HAPPINESS IS WHEN**
**WHAT YOU THINK,**
**WHAT YOU SAY**
**AND WHAT YOU DO**
**ARE ALL IN HARMONY"**
**MOHANDAS GANDHI**

## DAY 13. YOU ARE SO HAPPY THAT YOU ARE SPEAKING LIFE AND GIVING NO ROOM TO NEGATIVITY

I'm starting this section with a question **"How are you feeling?"**

I hope, desire, and pray that you are feeling happy today.

People search all over the world for happiness when happiness is already within all of us

Please read the quote again

**"HAPPINESS IS WHEN**
**WHAT YOU THINK,**
**WHAT YOU SAY**
**AND WHAT YOU DO**
**ARE ALL IN HARMONY"**
**MOHANDAS GANDHI**

I AM PERFECTLY AND WONDERFULLY MADE AND POWERFUL BEYOND MEASURE!

______________________________

(Don't forget to write down the above statement about you!)

**AM**

**IM SO HAPPY THAT I AM SPEAKING LIFE AND NOLONGER GIVING ROOM TO NEGATIVITY IN MY LIFE**

______________________________

______________________________

______________________________

You are on the journey to complete your purpose........ It's important to know:

**"When what you think, what you say, and what you do are in harmony..... Then you cannot help but feel happy". Mohandas Gandhi**

Think about this........

Before you took the time to think about and appreciate your past,

You may not have felt unhappy. Why?

1. Could it be because what you were doing (before my book) did not match what you thought you should be doing

Did you answer yes to that question?

If any of your thoughts does not match the feeling of happiness you have recently obtained....... then no matter when it happens........ I want you to instantly remember it is just a feeling

I AM PERFECTLY AND WONDERFULLY MADE AND POWERFUL BEYOND MEASURE!

---

(Don't forget to write down the above statement about you!)

YOU ARE POWERFUL AND YOU CAN CHANGE YOUR FEELINGS AT ANYTIME

Please know by now beyond a shadow of a doubt when that unhappy feeling comes in.......you have the ability to turn that feeling right back off

KEEP IN MIND **YOU DESERVE HAPPINESS**

Did you notice I didn't talk about the negative that may have come at you today?

Always positive never negative... but I didn't talk about it because you now have the tools to deal with whatever comes your way.

Negative things only makes you stronger, don't give any energy to anything negative and you will be OK.

When something negative is brought to you I only want you to evaluate the person who brought it.

It may be time to put them on notice because today you are happy and there is nothing they can do about it.

Remember on your purpose completing journey you cannot afford to entertain anybody negative.

I AM PERFECTLY AND WONDERFULLY MADE AND POWERFUL BEYOND MEASURE!

(Don't forget to write down the above statement about you!)

**PM**

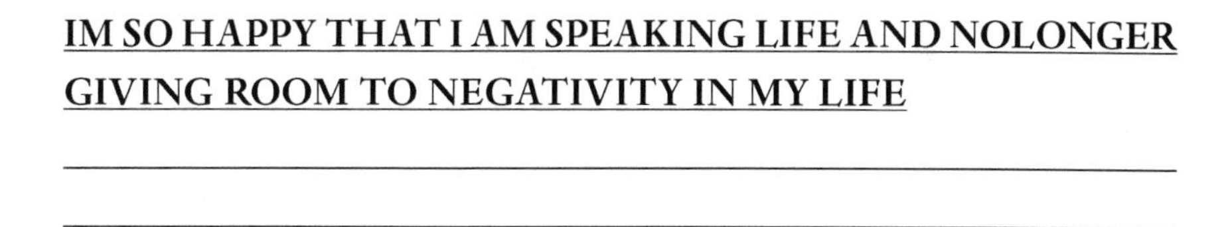

**IM SO HAPPY THAT I AM SPEAKING LIFE AND NOLONGER GIVING ROOM TO NEGATIVITY IN MY LIFE**

**Remember family....... say this statement all day every day, say it when anything negative creeps into your mind and say it when anyone says anything different about you.**

(Don't forget to write down the above statement about you!)

# DAY 14

# YOU ARE REALIZING WHY YOU ARE NEEDED SO MUCH IN THIS WORLD TODAY

**"NOT ALL OF THE PUZZLE**
**PIECES OF LIFE SEEM TO**
**FIT TOGATHER AT FIRST**
**BUT, IN TIME, YOU'LL FIND THEY**
**DID SO PERFECTLY"**
**DEE ZANTAMATA**

## DAY 14. YOU ARE REALIZING WHY YOU ARE NEEDED SO MUCH IN THIS WORLD TODAY

Now that you are happy, working on your purpose daily and never focusing on the negative aspects of your life. You should have a feeling of how much the world needed you to change.

The world was just waiting for you to stop living in the past and recognized your own personal the strength.

It took real strength to overcome what you have gone through in your life.

You like so many people didn't take the time to realize:

1. You will have never known how strong you were if you did not have to show strength at some point in your life.

(Don't forget to write down the above statement about you!)

2. You would have never known how forgiving you were if you didn't have to forgive someone or something done to you at some point in your life.
3. You would never have known how much you are needed if you didn't start loving the person you have become.

I want you take some time today to realize that your purpose is needed in the world we live in.

Visualize your purpose, how it's helping people and how your life has changed the moment your purpose was complete.

You cannot give up on your purpose or delay completing your purpose any longer.

I don't care what your purpose is...... whether it's an idea, a business, an invention, a product or service, whatever it is........

If the vision of your completed purpose has come to you then your purpose is needed. That's it that's all.

Shouting with my loud voice" **I NEED YOU AND YOUR PURPOSE**".

We were born to contribute to the world we have been blessed to live in. Your purpose is needed. You are in the final stretch complete your purpose please.

I AM PERFECTLY AND WONDERFULLY MADE AND POWERFUL BEYOND MEASURE!

______________________________________________

(Don't forget to write down the above statement about you!)

**AM**

**"TODAY I'M REALIZING WHY MY PURPOSE IS NEEDED SO MUCH IN THIS WORLD I LIVE IN".**

______________________________________________

______________________________________________

______________________________________________

I told you earlier in the book we are all pieces of a puzzle if you don't complete your purpose your piece is missing.

You've been doing 5 things a day so for some of you your purpose is already here.

You may have encountered some resistance to your new idea of goal but it's too late your purpose was completed by default the moment you visualized it in your mind.

You may be thinking my completed purpose doesn't seem like it fits in with the ideas of others but (think about this) before you let the negative thought creep in.

All the greatest inventors.......all the greatest contributors of our time...... were told their piece of the puzzle didn't fit just because it was new and different.

Henry Ford, Albert Einstein, Steve Jobs all were told that their puzzle piece did not fit at the time.

I AM PERFECTLY AND WONDERFULLY MADE AND POWERFUL BEYOND MEASURE!

---

(Don't forget to write down the above statement about you!)

Research their stories (any one of them) and see how many NO's they received before they received their YES.

People could not see their vision. But we all know that their puzzle pieces did fit.....

They all have a documented position in history but what if they stopped because of what people thought about their completed purpose?

I'm telling you..... Your piece (your completed purpose) is exactly what this world needs right now.

The time of invention, leadership, compassion, and understanding is passing us by.

THE WORLD NEEDS YOU.

We need the next idea, the next, invention, the next book, the next provider, the next leader, the next giver, the next contributor,

We need you to leave your legacy...... make your mark.....and take your documented place in history.

**YOU ARE NEEDED JUST LOOK AROUND.**

I AM PERFECTLY AND WONDERFULLY MADE AND POWERFUL BEYOND MEASURE!

________________________________________________

(Don't forget to write down the above statement about you!)

**PM**

**"TODAY I'M REALIZING WHY MY PURPOSE IS NEEDED SO MUCH IN THIS WORLD I LIVE IN".**

________________________________________________

________________________________________________

________________________________________________

**Remember family……. say this statement all day every day, say it when anything negative creeps into your mind and say it when anyone says anything different about you.**

I AM PERFECTLY AND WONDERFULLY MADE AND POWERFUL BEYOND MEASURE!

______________________________________________

(Don't forget to write down the above statement about you!)

# DAY 15

## YOU LOVE THE FACT THAT YOU DON'T SWEAT THE SMALL STUFF

**"WHEN YOU LOOK AT YOURSELF FROM A UNIVERSAL STANDPOINT, SOMETHING INSIDE ALWAYS REMINDS OR INFORMS YOU THAT THERE ARE BIGGER AND BETTER THINGS TO WORRY ABOUT"**
**ALBERT EINSTEIN**

### DAY 15- YOU LOVE THE FACT THAT YOU DON'T SWEAT THE SMALL STUFF

Its day 15 yea! Another key to unlocking your purpose is to remember never to sweat the small stuff.

I WANT TO INTRODUCE THE NEW YOU AGAIN

IT'S DAY 15……..

YOU ARE NOW **A POSITIVE PROFESSIONAL**

**AM**

**"TODAY I LOVE THE FACT THAT I DON'T SWEAT THE SMALL STUFF".**

______________________________________________

______________________________________________

______________________________________________

(Don't forget to write down the above statement about you!)

Whenever you set your mind and energy on a prize there will always be little things that come up.

The key to getting past the obstacles in your life is to never sweat the small stuff.

Some little.....well most...... of these obstacles will be caused by people and you can't change people but you can change their requirements for remaining in your circle.

Repeat...YES....NOW GET THIS PART

Today and every day you must learn to be grateful and not be moved by small things that may come up daily.

You're a pro now.....Small things will **come up**........ But my question to you is.......

What you will allow to **come down** in your response?

A positive professional never allows anger to come down, never allows frustration to come out, and never never gives up on their purpose.

It's not that you won't have negative days because I promise you will...... but a positive professional takes every negative thought and turns it to a positive thought.

1. A positive professional learns when to take breaks. Go outside and come back to it when you have created the atmosphere you want to be in.

(Don't forget to write down the above statement about you!)

2. A professional learns when to turn on the ocean sounds and reflects on just being grateful.
3. A positive professional utilizes the tools he or she has. Whatever step in my book you want to pull out to get you past the small things that seem so huge at times… use them

Some days there will be people sent solely to derail you off of the road to your completed purpose by any means necessary.

Small things will turn big things if you let it.

The key is to know any **small** thing left unhandled will turn into **big** thing.

**Please don't let it get big.**

Don't neglect any one on your purpose completing journey, don't neglect your job or your personal friendships on this road.

It's easy to become consumed by your vision but your friends, family, co-workers, need you also. Never sweat the small stuff but never turn your back on the small things either. They will get bigger I promise you.

I AM PERFECTLY AND WONDERFULLY MADE AND POWERFUL BEYOND MEASURE!

___

(Don't forget to write down the above statement about you!)

**PM**

**"TODAY I LOVE THE FACT THAT I DON'T SWEAT THE SMALL STUFF".**

___

___

___

**Remember family....... say this statement all day every day, say it when anything negative creeps into your mind and say it when anyone says anything different about you.**

I AM PERFECTLY AND WONDERFULLY MADE AND POWERFUL BEYOND MEASURE!

______________________________________________________________

(Don't forget to write down the above statement about you!)

## DAY 16

## YOU ARE SHOWING OTHER PEOPLE LOVE

**"I FEEL THAT THERE IS NOTHING MORE TRULY ARTISTIC THAN TO LOVE PEOPLE"**
**VINCENT VAN GOGH**

### DAY 16-YOU ARE SHOWING OTHER PEOPLE LOVE

It's time to show other people love.

These are some of the final keys a lot of this book was dedicated to you

Keeping your mind right, remaining grateful, focusing on the positive and focusing on completing your purpose.

Now I want to shift.....

I'm going to require you to focus on someone other than **yourself** today.

This book is an example of this very step. I would have never sat down and wrote this book to you if I stayed focused on me.

**AM**

**"TODAY I AM GOING TO SHOW OTHER PEOPLE LOVE".**

______________________________________________________________

______________________________________________________________

______________________________________________________________

(Don't forget to write down the above statement about you!)

You have to be a person that contributes to loving someone else or showing someone else love from time to time.

This section is designed not only to propel you to love the people in your circle but make sure that the people you say you love....... Know......Feel.....and understand why you love them.

This should be your first goal.

This seems like this is an easy goal but some of you have taken the people in your circle for granted. I just know it.

Especially when you started working on completing your purpose, it's easy to get side tracked and spend countless hours on research or just feeding yourself with positive thoughts.

Making that shift to being a positive professional is full time and has led to days of just spending time by yourself.

I know it's necessary (the countless hours mediating or working on your purpose) but I also know how the people who you love may be feeling

**Repeat......**

**If the people you say you love......Don't ....... Know......, Feel..... and understand why you love them. Then your journey to mend that relationship starts today.**

Add "show someone that I love them" to your list of the things you must complete daily.

---

(Don't forget to write down the above statement about you!)

Show them today...... tell them that you love and appreciate them.

Who are the people that you have to remind you love them.

1. Name ____________________
2. Name ____________________
3. Name ____________________
4. Name ____________________
5. Name ____________________

I always whispered in there ear of my children before they went to sleep or sometimes when they were already sleep. "MOMMY LOVES YOU I WILL ALWAYS LOVE MY BABY GIRL OR BOY'.

I now tell my grandchildren that same statement NA NA LOVES YOU I WILL ALWAYS LOVE MY BABY GIRL OR BOY'.

My children are grown now and we have had our ups and downs mainly because I'm not their friend I'm their mother.

If they cannot abide by the rules in my house then they simply cannot come.

So I taught them if you can't respect someone's house then you should not enter their house.

THIS WAS FREE AND ONE OF THE SIDE NOTES FOR PARENTS who think that their children are their friends.......

My opinion.....Get a friend and be a mother or father.....It's easier in the long run...trust me.

(Don't forget to write down the above statement about you!)

Every time my grown children would spend the night..... I still would whisper those same words I their ear; I wanted my family to know they were loved.

I also showed my children love even when I did not always agree with their choices

One thing was for sure their choices were not going to stop my love for them. I loved them before they were ever born and I never wanted them to experience the feeling of not being loved.

**Loving others is a requirement for you getting the opportunity to complete your purpose .**

Loving your family that's the easy part for some of you but I cannot give you easy without giving you something hard.......still very necessary.

This section is dedicated to you loving people who may have hurt you or loving perfect strangers.

You are the one that wants your dream, your purpose, or your desires right?

Well there is something's you may have to fix.

Loving people I feel is a requirement to obtaining not just your purpose but the riches that will come along with completing your purpose.

1. I told you we are connected and I need you to fix your love relationships

(Don't forget to write down the above statement about you!)

2. I need you to love strangers
3. I need you to love the people who hurt you because your purpose has been held up long enough.

And I need you to remember to love yourself through this process.

This spreading love exercise sometimes can bring up some feelings that you thought were buried.

Those negative feelings are not buried they just needed to be replaced with love feelings.

For some on you this part is what the world has been waiting for you to do finally.

The world was waiting for you to love and to forgive so the door that unlocks your completed purpose would be open to you.

Love in spite of....... Love leads you to grace .......and some of those doors I talked about on day 12 will be unlocked....... without a key.

THAT'S HOW POWERFUL LOVE IS.

This family is an important day...... so remember....... I love you and you must give love to someone today!

I AM PERFECTLY AND WONDERFULLY MADE AND POWERFUL BEYOND MEASURE!

(Don't forget to write down the above statement about you!)

**PM**

**"TODAY I SHOWED OTHER PEOPLE LOVE".**

**Remember family....... say this statement all day every day, say it when anything negative creeps into your mind and say it when anyone says anything different about you.**

I AM PERFECTLY AND WONDERFULLY MADE AND POWERFUL BEYOND MEASURE!

---

(Don't forget to write down the above statement about you!)

# DAY 17

# YOU ARE SPEAKING POSITIVE ABOUT ALL THINGS

**"FOCUS ON GOOD THOUGHTS AND GOOD THINGS WILL HAPPEN"**
**UNKNOWN AUTHOR**

## DAY 17-YOU ARE SPEAKING POSITIVE ABOUT ALL THINGS

Today is the day that you're speaking positive about everything that happens to you today.

This is an exercise that I want you to do periodically.

I want you to add to your daily to do list on Thursday, Friday, etc., I going to be positive about everything that happens to me on that day,

It's a test to see if you can really do what few men or women have been able to do.

It is easy to get caught up by what your boss, spouse, kids, news, friend, or family are doing and never really look at what you are personally doing.

Today I want you to write down what life through at you and I want you to write something positive on the other side as your response to what happen.

**YOU'RE THE POSITIVE PROFESSIONAL RIGHT!**

(Don't forget to write down the above statement about you!)

I give you an example below

Remember negatively delays YOU and if you stay on that point long enough is sucks the gas out of your gas tank and your car is broke down on the side of the road again.

We can't let that happen...... so right now focus on good thoughts and good things will happen.
STAY POSITIVE, THINK POSITIVE, AND DO POSITIVE.

**AM**

**"TODAY I AM SPEAKING POSITIVE ABOUT ALL THINGS".**

## STAY POSITIVE NEVER NEGATIVE!

| WHAT HAPPEN | POSITIVE THOUGHT |
| --- | --- |
| YOUR MATE IS MAD | YOU LEARNED SOMETHING NEW AND CHANGED FOR THE BETTER |
| YOUR CHECK IS LATE | YOU STILL HAD FOOD IN THE REFRIGERATOR |
| YOUR CAR BROKE DOWN | YOU STILL HAD THE ABILTY TO WALK OR RIDE THE TRAIN TO WORK |
| YOU HAVE A HEAD ACHE | YOU LIED DOWN OR TOOK A ASPRIN AND YOUR BETTER |

(Don't forget to write down the above statement about you!)

| WHAT HAPPEN | POSITIVE THOUGHT |
|---|---|
| YOU SAW SOMETHING NEGATIVE ON TV | YOU PRAYED FOR THE SITUATION AND SENT POSITIVE WAVES |

Those things happen every day.

Remember **nothing new** under the sun but make sure your response is always different. POSITIVE

Do you remember I told you when I gave money away I attach a change prayer to my money and if they took my money they took my power I associated with my money?

You must learn no matter what comes to you to only focus on the positive aspects of it.

MAN!................I have seen some stuff...... just by me being a black women and the mother of a black child that I could participated in the negative talk or protest but I refused.

**NEVER NEGATIVE ONLY POSITIVE**.

I believe that by me staying true to myself (positive professional) and sending my prayers instead of negative energy

I believe that **one less** person got hurt in the protest, **one less** person got killed in war, **one less** person experienced hate all because I refused to focus or give any of my energy to negatively.

(Don't forget to write down the above statement about you!)

Think about how many people you can save just by sending positive thoughts through the airwaves.

You cannot utilize your positive power unless you master the little things that give you the opportunity to see positive in the negative things that happen to you on a daily basis.

I need all of us to get to the point of using the positive power instead of negative conversation and our world would be a better place

I'm going to shift again but I need you to realize how much power your mind carries.

Right now most men and women are using the power of the mind to unlock riches.

I don't blame them because I need them to show you that you have that same power……. Most people would never try something new unless it was done before

When you tap into and use your power for good….WOW all I can say is WOW

Use your power to save, to heal, and to stop negative things from hurting so many people ……. that's the day I'm waiting for.

I need you to see the positive in all things that come your way daily and your personal power will get stronger and stronger.

I AM PERFECTLY AND WONDERFULLY MADE AND POWERFUL BEYOND MEASURE!

______________________________________________

(Don't forget to write down the above statement about you!)

**PM**

**"TODAY I AM SPEAKING POSITIVE ABOUT ALL THINGS".**

______________________________________________

______________________________________________

______________________________________________

**Remember family……. say this statement all day every day, say it when anything negative creeps into your mind and say it when anyone says anything different about you.**

I AM PERFECTLY AND WONDERFULLY MADE AND POWERFUL BEYOND MEASURE!

________________________________________

(Don't forget to write down the above statement about you!)

# DAY 18

## YOU ARE SEEING THE DIFFERENCE IN HOW PEOPLE VIEW YOU

**"PROMISE ME YOU'LL ALWAYS REMEMBER**
**YOU'RE BRAVER THAN YOU BELIEVE,**
**AND STRONGER THEN YOU SEEM,**
**AND SMARTER THAN YOU THINK"**
**AA MILNE**

### DAY 18-YOU ARE SEEING THE DIFFERENCE IN HOW PEOPLE VIEW YOU

You did it… you are now on the right road…… and you are starting to notice that people are treating you different

It's a feeling you receive when people start to see the difference in you.

Day 18 ……Receive a feeling of being proud of the changes you have made in your life.

**AM**

**"TODAY I SAW THE DIFFERENCE IN HOW PEOPLE VIEW ME".**

________________________________________

________________________________________

________________________________________

I AM PERFECTLY AND WONDERFULLY MADE AND POWERFUL BEYOND MEASURE!

---

(Don't forget to write down the above statement about you!)

It's time for me to tell a truth........my book is almost over and I have to make a confession to you (my reader)

I alluded to it in the beginning of the book that I did no always make the right choices well I did not always chose the right words.

I was a person who **used choice bad words** better than the average person when I got angry.

I used to think there were just certain situations where a bad word was deserved by the people who pissed me off.

I used to make up cuss words. Needless to say my purpose was delayed.

There is no room for negatively and there is no situation where a cuss word is required.

I learned the hard way.

When you cuss all the time there will be a time when you embarrass yourself.

Imagine being at work or at church....and cuss.

What you practice or do normally will always come out when you least expect it

So there I am at work and what happened? A cuss word comes out.

---

(Don't forget to write down the above statement about you!)

It was still a good thing……I was in management so to my employees it was funny; somehow it made me more approachable. I know it's weird

But I'm trying to make a point

Office meetings are not the times to be using profanity but that day happen to be my Day 17 where I was speaking positive about everything that happens to me.

I told you these steps were used by me first….. I had to make sure they worked.

On that day I made a vow that I was not going to cuss anymore.

Always honest, I cuss a couple thousand times after that day but today I'm proud to say I don't cuss as much as I used to.

I'm not that good it's not I became a master communicator I just removed the people who gave me the desire to want to cuss out of my life.

Focus….Sometimes you have to protect the anointing by any means necessary

Some on you are beating yourself up because you are doing the very thing that you do not want to do.

Don't make it that difficult

(Don't forget to write down the above statement about you!)

Change the things you can change....PROTECT THE NEW YOU!

1. If you used to drink stay away from liquor stores and bars.
2. If you used gossip don't answer your phone when you have those gossip feelings
3. If you are a little loose, don't speak to the opposite sex after 10:00pm
4. If you used drugs, stay away from users or places where drugs are sold
5. If you cuss, stay away from people and situations that upset you

**I just think there are some things that you can do to protect the new you**

**Now back to my original point**

My joy did not come from me not cussing anymore.

Actually not cussing frustrated me even more because I was still having the same moments but those moments lead me to using my right ear switch more and more until I changed my circle.

I'm telling you the things outlined in my book works......

Try to see the positive in everything and you will change for the better faster.

My joy came when my husband and my children said I cannot believe you did not go off, I can't believe you did not cuss I know you are mad as fish grease.

I AM PERFECTLY AND WONDERFULLY MADE AND POWERFUL BEYOND MEASURE!

___

(Don't forget to write down the above statement about you!)

Now I was mad but my greatest joy came because they (my family) noticed the change in me.

You should desire for your love ones to recognize the changes you have made.

You should want to be viewed by your peers in a positive manner.

If you are not **currently viewed in a positive manner** then you're just reading and not doing the things listed in this book.

If you were really doing the things listed in my book your purpose would have appeared by default and how people view you as a person would have changed by default.

If you have to change your public image...... then change it. Now

You cannot please everyone but you can allow people to see the new you and be thankful when they comment about you or notice the change.

**PM**

**"TODAY I SAW THE DIFFERENCE IN HOW PEOPLE VIEW ME".**

___

___

___

**Remember family....... say this statement all day every day, say it when anything negative creeps into your mind and say it when anyone says anything different about you.**

I AM PERFECTLY AND WONDERFULLY MADE AND POWERFUL BEYOND MEASURE!

______________________________________________

(Don't forget to write down the above statement about you!)

# DAY 19

# YOU ARE FEELING GREAT ABOUT YOURSELF

**"TODAY YOU ARE YOU,**
**THAT IS TRUER THAN TRUE.**
**THERE IS NO ONE ALIVE**
**WHO IS YOUER THAN YOU"**
**DR. SEUSS**

## DAY 19- YOU ARE FEELING GREAT ABOUT YOURSELF

It's almost over; I may have lost some of you along the way because you could not believe it was that's simple. But if you are still reading I'm talking to you.

Today you are feeling great about yourself.

So many of us feel great about other people and never take the time to feel great about ourselves.

**AM**

**"TODAY I FEEL GREAT ABOUT MYSELF".**

______________________________________________

______________________________________________

______________________________________________

I AM PERFECTLY AND WONDERFULLY MADE AND POWERFUL BEYOND MEASURE!

---

(Don't forget to write down the above statement about you!)

Yes this section is dedicated to you:

You are perfectly and wonderfully made

You are loved and needed.

I wrote this book to encourage you along your purpose completing journey.

I don't care what you are going through today I want you to know you are GREAT and I am feeling good about the new you.

I feel overjoyed about the real you....the person who is on day or step 19 of my book.

I love you so much and I am sending encouragement right now.

This section alone is pushing you out of your down feelings and propelling you back into the feelings conveyed throughout this whole book.

If you are not feeling great, absolutely great about yourself then know there is someone in California who feel so great about you that tears are running down my face even writing those words.

If you are not feeling great today about you and you alone I want you to STOP READING AND GO BACK TO THE TOP OF THIS BOOK.

I AM PERFECTLY AND WONDERFULLY MADE AND POWERFUL BEYOND MEASURE!

________________________________________________

(Don't forget to write down the above statement about you!)

REMEMBER I DID NOT WRITE THIS BOOK TO ENTERTAIN YOU. I WROTE THIS BOOK TO GIVE YOU SOME KEYS HOPEFULLY THE RIGHT KEYS TO UNLOCK YOUR PURPOSE.

You are great, you are loved, you are needed, you are not who your past says you are, you are great. Today I need you to celebrate you in your sleep now.

When you go to sleep...go to sleep with the thought that you are great

**PM**

**"TODAY I FEEL GREAT ABOUT MYSELF".**

________________________________________________

________________________________________________

________________________________________________

**"TODAY YOU ARE GREAT,**
**AND THERE IS NOTHING THAT WILL HAPPEN**
**THAT CAN CHANGE THAT"**
**DANYELLE DICKSON**

Dig inside and be extraordinary today and every day for that matter!

**Remember family....... say this statement all day every day, say it when anything negative creeps into your mind and say it when anyone says anything different about you.**

I AM PERFECTLY AND WONDERFULLY MADE AND POWERFUL BEYOND MEASURE!

---

(Don't forget to write down the above statement about you!)

# DAY 20

## YOU ARE NOW SHARING WITH OTHERS

**"IT'S NOT HOW MUCH WE GIVE BUT HOW MUCH LOVE WE PUT INTO GIVING"**
**MOTHER TERESA**

### DAY 20- YOU ARE NOW SHARING WITH OTHERS

**THERES A SHARING PARTY GOING ON...... AND YOU ARE THE GUEST OF HONOR!**

It's your time to shine.

You truly shine by caring enough, being daring enough, and sharing your purpose with someone else.

You may have been secretly working on your purpose but today It's time to share your purpose with someone else.

**AM**

**"TODAY I WILL SHARE MY PURPOSE WITH SOMEONE".**

---

---

---

Chose this person wisely and share your purpose with someone you trust.

I AM PERFECTLY AND WONDERFULLY MADE AND POWERFUL BEYOND MEASURE!

---

(Don't forget to write down the above statement about you!)

This is an important step you cannot walk in fear and you must speak life into your purpose.

Sharing your purpose with others sets the atmosphere to being ready to receive and release your purpose to the world.

Before you do this step...... I caution you........ **Not** to put a time frame on the completion of your purpose just because you share your purpose with someone else.

I encourage you to tell the person who you are sharing your purpose with **not** to put a timeframe on your purpose either.

Before you tell them ask them to promise you somethings

1. Not to ask you over and over..... When is your purpose going to happen, or my favorite where are you at on that purpose of yours?
2. Tell them not to ask about your purpose over and over again.
3. Tell them not to share your idea with anyone else

I didn't do these steps before I shared my purpose and I regretted it.

My first book was called "SHUT YOUR MOUTH AND HEAR FROM GOD.

That book still has not been published yet but I wrote it in 2006, and I told everyone around me at the time.

I told my husband Ivan, my pastor at that time was Chris Esteeves, and even gave him a copy of my word document, shared it with my

(Don't forget to write down the above statement about you!)

friends Estelle Nelson and La Tanya Taylor(LT) and still today that book **HAS NOT BEEN** published **YET…**

**SMILE ITS COMING**

I tell myself daily that GOD plans are not my plans and he wanted my first book to be "I SEE YOU "but non-the less sharing with them gave me a multitude of negative feelings.

Sharing my purpose should have been a good thing but for years I carried around the feelings of procrastination, embracement, resentment,

Why did I have to open my big mouth?

I don't want you to have those feeling so whatever you do…**DON'T SKIP THIS STEP.**

Now you should be a lot closer to your purpose if you are completing 5 things every day you are miles ahead of where I was.

It's time to share your purpose, your dream, your invention, your purpose no matter what it is.

Once you share it……. go back to work……do the steps for your purpose to come to pass.

There is another requirement to sharing;

You shared your purpose so you must share love and understanding with someone else today.

I AM PERFECTLY AND WONDERFULLY MADE AND POWERFUL BEYOND MEASURE!

---

(Don't forget to write down the above statement about you!)

You must share anything that you have learned from this book or it may be time to share what you currently do with your replacement at your job.

Whatever you choose to share is up to you……but you must be a sharer.

Sharing with others will unlock the door to your purpose faster than you will ever know.

Share and be a person that others would love to share with you. Make sure you are a person that speaks life into whatever is being shared with you and they will give life back to your purpose.

**PM**

**"TODAY I SHARED MY PURPOSE WITH SOMEONE".**

---

---

---

**Remember family……. say this statement all day every day, say it when anything negative creeps into your mind and say it when anyone says anything different about you.**

I AM PERFECTLY AND WONDERFULLY MADE AND POWERFUL BEYOND MEASURE!

(Don't forget to write down the above statement about you!)

# DAY 21

## YOU ARE SPEAKING AND LIVING YOUR DREAM IN YOUR MIND AND WATCHING YOUR LIFE ALLIGN WITH YOUR WORDS

**"HAPPINESS IS WHEN WHAT YOU THINK, WHAT YOU SAY, AND WHAT YOU DO ARE IN HARMONY"**
**MOHANDAS GANDHI**

## DAY 21- YOU ARE SPEAKING AND LIVING YOUR DREAM IN YOUR MIND AND WATCHING YOUR LIFE ALLIGN WITH YOUR WORDS

You made it you completed all 21 days. I'm so proud of you.

I know I said it before in the beginning of this book but I just have to say it again

1. I loved you,……I really do
2. I needed you….I really do,
3. You were born with your purpose…..You really were
4. You and only you have the blue print to unlock that purpose….You really do

**NOW LOOK AT YOU**

I AM PERFECTLY AND WONDERFULLY MADE AND POWERFUL BEYOND MEASURE!

______________________________________________________________

(Don't forget to write down the above statement about you!)

AM

**"TODAY I AM SPEAKING AND LIVING MY DREAMS IN MY MIND AND WATCHING MY LIFE ALLIGN WITH MY THOUGHTS AND MY WORDS".**

______________________________________________________________

______________________________________________________________

______________________________________________________________

**You are a different person,**

Today you are a person that knows.... You are perfectly and wonderfully made,
Today you are a person that knows.....You are great,
Today you are a person that.................Always focusses on the good
Today you are a person that.................Has forgiven not only yourself but others,
Today you are a person that................ Is grateful,
Today you are a person who takes each day as a gift (another chance to get it right)
Today you are a person who does 5 things everyday towards completing your purpose
Today you are a person that is sharing and attaching a positive seed to everyone you sow into.

**Today........ I'm just a proud family member,**

I'm proud of the person you are today but I'm even prouder of all the accomplishments that will come out of you from this day forward.

I AM PERFECTLY AND WONDERFULLY MADE AND POWERFUL BEYOND MEASURE!

______________________________________________

(Don't forget to write down the above statement about you!)

Remember this exercise:

***I __________ (your name) will accomplish _________ (your purpose or goal)by date _____________ and once I accomplish this I will make ______________ (specific dollar amount). I will give ______________ (what your are going to give back) in return for allowing me to accomplish my purpose.***

***I thank you so much for allowing me to contribute to this world and I will give my talents back to the world to help someone else before I die. (Say and write this statement somewhere that you can see it at all times.)***

***I want you to send yourself and email or text that says this very statement every night before you go to bed. And the first text or email you read will be you promise to yourself and to the world.***

***You wrote down and spoke your dream, your desire, your goal or your purpose and now you are living your dreams because all the work you completed.***

**<u>Again I'm proud of you...Thank you for reading my completed purpose</u>.**

**<u>PM</u>**

**<u>"TODAY I AM SPEAKING AND LIVING MY DREAMS IN MY MIND AND WATCHING MY LIFE ALLIGN WITH MY THOUGHTS AND MY WORDS".</u>**

______________________________________________

______________________________________________

______________________________________________

I AM PERFECTLY AND WONDERFULLY MADE AND POWERFUL BEYOND MEASURE!

---

(Don't forget to write down the above statement about you!)

**Remember family……. say this statement all day every day, say it when anything negative creeps into your mind and say it when anyone says anything different about you.**

**"THE FUTURE BELONGS**
**TO THOSE WHO**
**BELIEVE IN THE BEAUTY OF THEIR DREAMS"**
**ELEANOR ROOSEVELT**

***So let's summarize this section:***

YOUR WERE BORN WITH A PURPOSE

\+

YOU HAD EVERTHINNG AT BIRTH YOU
NEEDED TO FULLFILL THAT PURPOSE

=

YOU HAVE COMPLETED
THE STEPS REQUIRED
AND
NOW
YOU HAVE

=

(Don't forget to write down the above statement about you!)

# Completion of your purpose

**It's done!**

**You have completed your purpose!**

**IF I DIE TOMORROW GOD WANTED ME TO SHARE THIS BOOK WITH YOU TODAY**

I DANYELLE DICKSON REALLY SEE YOU

TO EVERYONE THAT WILL EVER READ THIS BOOK:

**I SEE YOU**
**YOU HAVE NOW SEEN YOUR DESTINY,**
**YOU HAVE WROTE DOWN**
**YOUR DREAM OR DESIRES**
**YOU HAVE LEARNED**
**WHAT WAS REQUIRED TO**
**ACCOMPLISH YOUR DREAM,**

(Don't forget to write down the above statement about you!)

**YOU WERE THANKFUL FOR**
**EVERY OBSTACLE THAT YOU**
**ENCOUNTERED ALONG THE WAY,**
**YOU GAVE TO OTHERS WHILE**
**YOU WERE COMPLETING**
**YOUR JOURNEY,**
**YOU ARE FULFILLING AND**
**LIVING YOUR PURPOSE,**
**YOU ARE SHARING WITH OTHERS**
**YOU ARE LEARNING**
**YOU ARE REACHING YOUR GOALS**
**YOU ARE CONTRIBUTING**
**TO OUR FAMILY WORLDWIDE!**
**I SEE YOU AND THANK YOU**
**FOR ACCOMPLISHING YOUR**
**GOAL OR PURPOSE**
**OUR WORLD NEEDED YOU!**

**"GO CONFIDENTLY IN**
**THE DIRECTION**
**OF YOUR DREAMS!**

I AM PERFECTLY AND WONDERFULLY MADE AND POWERFUL BEYOND MEASURE!

---

(Don't forget to write down the above statement about you!)

## LIVE THE LIFE YOU'VE IMAGINED"
## THOREAU

# THIS BOOK IS DEDICATED TO CELEBRATING THE NEW YOU

# ABOUT THE AUTHOR

Danyelle Dickson is one of the most passionate personal development trainers of our time.

After growing up in foster homes and working in Corporate America she states one day she woke up and realized her gifts and talents were being used up by an billion dollar company and she just wanted to help people before she died.

Danyelle is one women committed to never speaking negative only positive about all things we encounter in life.

Danyelle's believes her gift to the world (her mark that she was here) is her book **I SEE YOU A 21 day Journey To Help You Unlock Your Purpose.**

Danyelle hopes her book compels you (her readers) to speak positive always and live your life you were born to live

Danyelle has a GOD given talent to motivate, encourage, and inspire people all over the world not to look at their current circumstances however look at the blessing of receiving another new day.

Danyelle quit her job to make the world her employer and will not waste another day not doing what she was born to do.

Danyelle's is on a World Wide Survivor Mission to pick men and women up from the depths of their past and lift them to the heights of their future.

Danyelle has created "5 DAILY STEPS" and this process has become legendary for personal development programs, network marketing programs and workshops across the world.

To book Danyelle Dickson for your event, call, or workshop email her at

successwithdanyelle@gmail.com

Sometimes you can see love
even when your eyes are closed......
Mr. and Mrs. Ivan Dickson.....
WE SEE YOU AND LOVE YOU!

Printed in the United States
By Bookmasters